REMEMBER,
Every
Breath
is Precious

Merry Christmas

Jo Ellen

All My Love,

Donna

2019

REMEMBER,
Every
Breath
is Precious

Dying Taught Me How to Live

by

Lesley Joan Lupo

www.whitecrowbooks.com

Praise for

Remember, Every Breath is Precious.

In this wonderful and inspiring book, Lesley Lupo writes in detail about her deep near-death experience (NDE), while visiting "Upstairs" due to a severe cerebral trauma. Her healing unexpectedly surpassed the doctor's predictions, but in the first months after her coma, her total failure to remember anything else in her life terrified her. Luckily for us, she could describe her overwhelming and inspiring experience, with the meeting of light beings that revealed wisdom, compassion, devotion, ultimate truth and unconditional love, and with her decision to come back in her damaged body. Her NDE is one of the most impressive and detailed experiences I have ever read. She was unable to share her knowledge with others because words utterly fail in a description, and no one would listen. So her life was at first very difficult, but she could not forget her ultra-real experience, and at last, she no longer denied her spiritual path or her inborn gifts. Little by little, she started to integrate her awakened immortal soul with her ordinary waking consciousness, and she is now able to describe for us her tremendous personal and spiritual growth. This book is an excellent gift for anyone who is willing to be open to their spiritual aspects, and who is willing to help to shift personal and global consciousness. Highly recommended.

~ **PIM VAN LOMMEL,** CARDIOLOGIST, NDE-RESEARCHER,
AUTHOR OF *CONSCIOUSNESS BEYOND LIFE.*

Many books can be found today that recount vivid, emotionally gripping tales of near-death experiences and meetings with spirits. You will find such an account in *Remember, Every Breath is Precious.* But author Lesley Joan Lupo, who had the NDE, then goes in a new and exceedingly valuable direction. She is aware how strange NDEs can seem when compared with our everyday experiences, so she investigated her experience from several fresh angles. The result is additional layers of evidence indicating that something exceedingly strange did indeed happen. A compelling, original work.

~ **DEAN RADIN**, AUTHOR OF *REAL MAGIC; ANCIENT WISDOM, MODERN SCIENCE, AND A GUIDE TO THE SECRET POWER OF THE UNIVERSE.*

Lesley's fascinating descriptions of what 'the Other Side' was like for her contain many life-enhancing benefits for YOU here and now. Her unique perspective after visiting 'Upstairs' provides wise answers to many questions you have likely pondered. Despite researching afterlife topics for over forty years, I learned a lot from *Remember, Every Breath is Precious* and highly recommend you do the same.

~ **MARK PITSTICK, MA, DC,** ETERNEA DIRECTOR OF EDUCATION AND AUTHOR OF *SOUL PROOF.*

Remember, Every Breath is Precious is a very personal and courageous book. The reader will especially enjoy how Lesley Lupo included veridical evidence—from an evidential medium to an astrology reading of the exact date of the accident in the appendices. Anyone interested in how NDEs relate to our ability to transform our consciousness and express our true potential should enjoy this book.

~ **RAJIV PARTI, MD.,** AUTHOR OF DYING TO WAKE UP

Lesley Lupo's *Remember, Every Breath is Precious* is a stirring and well-written account of her fascinating near-death experience. Her book is one of the most engaging and engrossing I have had the pleasure to read on this subject. Be prepared to enjoy a real cover-to-cover page-turner; one which, I imagine, most readers will not want to put down.

~ **RAYMOND A. MOODY, JR., M.D., PH.D.,** AUTHOR OF *LIFE AFTER LIFE*

When Lesley Lupo had her near-death experience in 1988, she did not merely encounter a heavenly light. No, she seems to have entered and remained in a heavenly realm, which she then is able to describe for the reader in stunning and thrilling detail. Thus her story is unique and uniquely valuable. In forty years of researching NDEs, I have never found so complete an account of what may await us after death. And that's just the beginning of her gripping and inspiring personal story in a book that is also full of the fruits of Lesley's hard-won spiritual wisdom. In short, this is one of those books that will leave an indelible mark on its readers. It certainly did on me.

~ **KENNETH RING, PH.D.,**
AUTHOR OF *LESSONS FROM THE LIGHT*

A brilliant, highly readable and extremely enlightening account of a life-transforming NDE—one that again demonstrates, and more clearly than ever, that we have a consciousness that is beyond our brain and beyond even our organic existence. A book to be read by everyone who ever doubted that this might be the case.

~ **ERVIN LASZLO, PH.D.,** AUTHOR OF *SCIENCE AND THE AKASHIC FIELD: AN INTEGRAL THEORY OF EVERYTHING*

When Lesley Lupo was thrown from her horse and crushed in a stampede, she left her body and was stunned to find that she was still herself, permeated by unconditional love, not because she had earned it but because that's just the way it is. The last thing she was told before she came back to a painful rehabilitation in this life was, "Remember, every breath is precious." In this book by that name, she shares her journey and the insights she gained. Readers will find this book not only a spellbinding narrative but also a practical guide to integrating spirituality into daily life.

~ **BRUCE GREYSON, M.D.,** PROFESSOR EMERITUS OF PSYCHIATRY, UNIVERSITY OF VIRGINIA SCHOOL OF MEDICINE; FOUNDER IANDS

Remember, Every Breath is Precious provides an engaging and moving account of one of the most detailed and profound Near-Death Experiences ever reported. The experience proved to be transformational for Lesley Lupo, and her masterful presentation of it in this inspiring text will be transformational for many others. This is an important book on many levels and a must-read for anyone interested in Near-Death Experiences and the wide-ranging opportunities that these phenomena provide for enhancing our understanding of ourselves and our universe.

~ **DAVID O. WIEBERS, M.D.,** AUTHOR OF *THEORY OF REALITY: EVIDENCE FOR EXISTENCE BEYOND THE BRAIN AND TOOLS FOR YOUR JOURNEY*

Life isn't a race, it is a pathway. From my own NDE and experience as a scientist and medium, I know that every word of Lesley's book is more than true. Lesley shares some of the best advice: "Just start from this position: every breath is precious. You are loved. Live the love you are in the now, and be ready for more to unfold. Have faith and slow yourself down. Add patience to your daily practices. Everything will work out for you, even if sometimes it doesn't look like it will. The Divine Upstairs has your back."

~ **DR. ALAN ROSS HUGENOT, ENGR.SC.D.,** AUTHOR OF *THE DEATH EXPERIENCE: WHAT IT IS LIKE WHEN YOU DIE*

Lesley shares the most in depth, beautifully written and detailed personal account of "Heaven" that I have had the pleasure to read. From her meeting with Jesus and His message of forgiveness to the reasons and purpose why we choose to incarnate on the earth, *Remember, Every Breath is Precious* is a must read for those who truly want to know what waits for them beyond the veil.

~ **VIRGINIA HUMMEL,** AUTHOR OF *CRACKING THE GRIEF CODE*

This gift of a book is not only a spectacular tour guide to Heaven, what Lesley calls "Upstairs", it is a portal to that realm. Reading the words, if you turn within, you will hear your soul whisper, 'Now do you remember?' Thank you, Lesley, for guiding us so lovingly back Home.

~ **SUZANNE GIESEMANN,** MEDIUM AND AUTHOR OF
MESSAGES OF HOPE

Lesley's clear and detailed account of her experience "Upstairs" is one more powerful confirmation that there are realities that lie beyond this world. While physics can provide a supportive framework in which other such realities can exist, there is nothing so compelling as a firsthand experience of these realms of joy and peace. Her book is also a powerfully moving tale of overcoming adversity that will give heart to anyone dealing with their own major challenges—and give them insights and tools to bring Divine awareness dynamically into how their lives unfold.

~ **JOSEPH SELBIE,** *THE PHYSICS OF GOD*

"Lesley's personal narrative of "Heaven" is gracefully written as it speaks to the heart and helps us to connect with our loved ones across the veil. Her encounter with Jesus is profound! As a nurse, I feel that Every Breath is Precious is truly spiritual medicine for the soul and a gift for those who genuinely seek answers to what happens when our Earthly journey ends."

~ **ERICA MCKENZIE, RN,** AUTHOR OF *DYING TO FIT IN.*

In this fascinating book, Lesley Lupo describes her extensive, near-death experience that resulted from being trampled by horses during a near fatal accident. The depth of subjective experience that Lesley described, occurring during a time when the injuries sustained led to her resuscitation being abandoned, defies materialist explanations. Lesley describes how her massive brain injury resolved in a remarkably short amount of time in comparison to the extent of her injury. This enthralling book details her incredible journey of physical and emotional healing that ensued thus enabling her to understand and integrate her experience. Due to her ongoing spiritual practice, Lesley regularly connects with the spiritual realm and her guides. This book is full of wisdom and insights revealed to Lesley during her experience and healing journey and this is something we can all benefit from without having to nearly die.

~ **PENNY SARTORI,** AUTHOR OF *THE TRANSFORMATIVE POWER OF NEAR-DEATH EXPERIENCES: HOW THE MESSAGES OF NDES CAN POSITIVELY IMPACT THE WORLD.*

Lesley Lupo's book *Remember, Every Breath is Precious* is a compelling account of her spiritual journey which began when she was a child and played with spirit guides who no one else in her family could see. Lesley's journey took a dramatically deeper turn during a near-death experience (NDE) that occurred after she was pushed by a frightened horse which then kicked and dragged her around the corral, resulting in a severe traumatic brain injury that caused her heart to stop beating. During the event, Lesley's awareness left her body and she entered a light-filled realm, which she calls "Upstairs," where she met her guides. In her time with them, she received many profound insights about the nature of life and death.

In Lesley's account she shares the fascinating wisdom she was taught "Upstairs" - how we plan our life trajectory in this world and the lessons we have to learn. She also tells of the terrifying moment during her recovery when the hospital physician told her, "If I hear that you have said even one more word [about it], I will transfer you to a psychiatric hospital for the rest of your recovery. I will pump you up with so many drugs that you will not know if it is day or night." This is a poignant reminder of the large gap that still exists between the materialist belief system of many clinicians in the medical profession and the often validated experiences of persons who have NDEs. One highlight of this book is the set of appendices, including the reading given to Lesley Lupo by the evidential medium Suzanne Giesemann, in which, without knowing any details of Lesley's NDE, she confirmed the events that had occurred on the other side.

I highly recommend this book, and the perspective it gives us about the preciousness of our life on this earth, as well as the profound support we always have from the loving beings on the other side. As the title says, "Remember, Every Breath is Precious."

~ **MARJORIE HINES WOOLLACOTT, PH.D.,** AUTHOR OF
INFINITE AWARENESS, THE AWAKENING OF A SCIENTIFIC MIND

For information, contact White Crow Books
at 3 Hova Villas, Hove, BN3 3DH United Kingdom,
or e-mail info@whitecrowbooks.com.

Cover Design by Astrid@Astridpaints.com
Interior design by Velin@Perseus-Design.com

Paperback ISBN 978-1-78677-069-1
eBook   ISBN 978-1-78677-070-7

Non-Fiction / Body, Mind & Spirit / Parapsychology / Near-Death Experience

www.whitecrowbooks.com

CONTENTS

Suddenly my conscious awareness, my soul,
popped out and stood ten feet away.
A thirty-six-year-old woman, "me,"
continued her attempts to wiggle in between
a wall of tightly packed horses.
Shocked, all I thought was "What the...?"

Where Science and Spirit Meet

Gary E. Schwartz, PhD

Most of us, when we die, remain "dead" physically. We are not given a "second chance" to return to our bodies and continue to live (physically) on the earth. However, some of us not only experience a physical death but discover a "greater reality" during the period when our hearts stop beating, and our brain waves have literally "flat-lined," showing no evidence of brain function. Furthermore, after we somehow returned to our physical bodies and recovered, we are given the profound opportunity to share with others what we witnessed and learned "on the other side."

You are about to read one of the most—if not "the" most—comprehensive, breathtaking, inspirational, humbling, and beautiful descriptions of what Lesley Lupo calls "upstairs," and others call "heaven." In fact, as you will see, *Every Breath is Precious* deserves to be among the most important books ever written about what it is like in the afterlife. The purpose of this foreword is not to reveal this profound information, but rather to help you understand why we should all ideally read this material with open and grateful minds and hearts.

There are now literally hundreds of books and articles published about such "near-death experiences" (NDE's). Some of these books have been major *New York Times* bestsellers, including *Proof of Heaven* by the former Harvard neurosurgeon Eben Alexander MD. In Alexander's case, he did not actually "die" so much as he endured a profound neurological disease (an extreme case of meningitis), which could have killed him or left him severely intellectually and emotionally impaired. Here is how his publisher described what happened:

> Alexander's recovery is by all accounts a medical miracle. But the real wonder of his story lies elsewhere. While his body lay in a coma, he journeyed beyond this world and encountered an angelic being who guided him into the deepest realms of super-physical existence. There he met and spoke with the Divine source of the universe itself.

Can Alexander's extraordinary account be right? Is Lesley Lupo's more extensive, more in-depth, and far-reaching narrative real?

Let me introduce myself. I am an academic scientist, a professor of psychology, medicine, neurology, psychiatry, and surgery at the University of Arizona, and director of the Laboratory for Advances in Consciousness and Health. I grew up in an atheist home, and my education entailed secular Western science and medicine. In my Ph.D. training at Harvard University, I learned that the brain created consciousness and that this was a scientifical fact. Like Alexander, for the first half of my academic career spanning twenty years at Harvard and Yale (1967 – 1988), I accepted mainstream science's explanation without reservations.

However, that was then, and this now. I have written about my unexpected scientific journey from being an education-based rejection of spirituality to developing and nurturing an evidence-based acceptance of the existence of a more significant spiritual reality over the course of seven books, culminating with *Synchronicity and the One Mind*. I share this professional background with you so that you can better understand, and appreciate, why I am actively endorsing Lesley Lupo's breakthrough book *Remember, Every Breath is Precious*. Here are the five primary reasons.

First, I have known Lesley for approximately twenty years. I met her a few years after the summer of 1989 when I began consulting at the Canyon Ranch health resort in Tucson. I was well aware of how respected she was (and is) by the founding executives at "the Ranch" (as we call it). Moreover, I have come to know Lesley particularly well over the past five years.

Our friendship includes our spending hundreds of hours in bi-weekly (on the average) science and spirit research meetings as well as giving many hours of collaborative presentations at the Ranch. Lesley also serves as an esteemed and well-respected member of the Circle of Trustees in my laboratory. Lesley's integrity and ethics are irreproachable.

Second, although Lesley's primary role at the Ranch is a guest services provider in its metaphysical department, Lesley is not a naïve and gullible spiritual believer. She is what I would term a "science-minded mystic." Lesley has had a long-standing passion for science; in fact, she regularly emails me current science articles that I should read. My training complements Lesley; I have been described as being an "intuitive-minded scientist." We launched a successful bi-monthly joint lecture named *Science and the Near-Death Experience*. Lesley now handles herself, but, in the beginning, our combined talk illustrates this complementarity.

Third, Lesley is an astute and careful observer. She pays close attention to details, and, thanks to the assistance of a long-time guest at the Ranch, Mr. Leslie Klein, she provided these details with clarity and beauty. Psychological research documents errors of cognition including confirmation biases and false memories. However, enough of Lesley's detailed descriptions have been independently validated to justify our giving Lesley the "benefit of the doubt." Consequently, we can comfortably read her observations and interpretations with an open mind and heart and then come to our conclusions.

Fourth, Lesley has authentic psychic capabilities. I have witnessed these gifts multiple times over the years, and they never cease to amaze me. A few months before I wrote this Foreword, I was having a Wednesday 3 p.m. meeting with Lesley at the Double U Café in Canyon Ranch. Stimulated by a surprising phrase she used in our conversation, I encouraged Lesley to use her mediumship skills (something she rarely does). To my amazement, Lesley ended up receiving highly accurate information regarding a famous deceased person who is associated with our ongoing after death communication research. Importantly, like most people at that time, Lesley was "blind" to this person's identity and his involvement in our ongoing investigation.

And, fifth, Lesley is evidence-based in her values and thinking. She is like a Sherlock Holmes of spiritual detection. You will read about my favorite evidential example toward the end of this book. Working with the distinguished medium Suzanne Giesemann who was blind to the details of Lesley's NDE, Suzanne ended up receiving confirmatory information about what Lesley experienced "Upstairs" in a manner that no honest skeptical person could deny. To the best of my knowledge, this is the first time in the history of this work that a research-oriented medium independently corroborated essential details of a person's NDE experience.

If we take all these five facts together, they provide a compelling case for our celebrating *Remember, Every Breath is Precious*. According to Lesley, it was while she was Upstairs that she heard the phrase "Where science and spirit meet." Thanks to Lesley's devotion and skills (and secondarily to Leslie's assistance), we can come to know this grand and unique meeting.

May you enjoy and grow from Lesley's journey as much as I have.

PREFACE

You are about to travel into a different world, a world that defies description; yet, to share this journey, describe it I must. Over the last few years, I have met many people who have also lived through a near-death experience (NDE). We all shake our heads and marvel at the wonders that we experienced; yet all share the same helpless frustration when we attempt to portray what we saw and felt during the journey. Describing the sensations and our full awareness of any spiritual experience is next to impossible—the words that we use pale in comparison to the majesty of the other side. Throughout the book, I will attempt to express what I find indescribable. Hampered by the tiny, little words that language gives us, I can only hope that you get a glimpse of what I saw.

Compare the differences you might experience if you stood on the rim of the Grand Canyon and viewed it firsthand with seeing the same place in a photograph. A two-dimensional picture cannot capture the splendor and magnificence of the canyon, yet that is all we are given to work with as we struggle to describe the events. I'm sorry I cannot give you a better picture, but when my emotions swell up and combine with the happiness of my memories, words seem like concrete: bulky, immovable, bland. They fail me.

In 1988, there were not a lot of books about NDEs available. For many years, I held my story inside, savoring it myself. People treated the subject, as if it had been a hallucination, two inches away from a psychotic break, nothing more. Back then I hadn't discovered Raymond Moody and his seminal work on people who had died and been resuscitated, *Life after Life*, where he coined the phrase *near-death experience*.

At that time, I was an agnostic bordering on atheist. I lived a good life, i.e., I had a conscience; I knew the difference between right and wrong and aimed to do the right thing. However, I did not have a certainty in the existence of God, the Unmanifest, or whatever names people use to describe a higher consciousness and an afterlife; I had no opinion or, frankly, any interest. Whether people go to Heaven or explode into particles of light were the same to me as if we dissolve at death. Spiritual matters held no significance in my daily life.

Then I was caught in a stampede of horses. After all that I went through, I could not return to a life devoid of my inner light. I found it. Perhaps I was a bit of a hard nut and needed a good *thunk* on the head, but I changed and was hungry to explore spiritual consciousness in all forms.

I think it more likely that as experiencers begin to commune with each other about our different journeys to Heaven, it will promote a broader comprehension of that precious and awe-inspiring spirit which connects us all. We all have the ability to encounter and brush up against the immense love and peacefulness, which is available to every single soul without having to endure such extreme circumstances. Because we are all such different vessels, we hold the energy in infinitely different ways. Competition on who "holds it correctly" is finally waning: differences between our perceptions are honored and enjoyed, not rejected. I have found that anyone who makes a blanket statement about the way of any spiritual path is speaking of *their* experience and innocently assuming that what works for me will surely work for you.

The herd instinct is in our hard wiring, strong and subliminal. The wiring for one leader originates in our animal brain. For millennia, this helped with our spiritual path. During the Egyptian dynasties, world populations were around twenty-seven million and it is estimated that in Egypt, there was between one and two million. It is much simpler to have everyone believe in a central, core belief if there aren't that many people, hence the ability to teach one pathway, one leader, one herd boss. Yet at that time, if someone held a different belief, one that was considered outside the norm, it appeared to endanger any groups' security. We had small enough tribes for leaders, champions, to be influential.

Around 1800, we hit one billion and have been skyrocketing ever since. Our challenge is to stop waiting for one person who will appeal to all seven billion plus people and link our arms together, relishing the differences between us rather trying to eradicate them.

In my acknowledgments, I express my gratitude to the people who helped me to polish this book. If it were not for their questions, I would not have realized that my first draft showed only the tip of the iceberg. I dived in and mapped out the rest of details to encompass the entire experience.

The pivotal person who inspired me and then doggedly urged me to sit down and "just do it" was Leslie Klein. Many years ago, I met him and his lovely wife, Janice. Moreover, of course, it worked out in a synchronistic manner. At a family wedding in Phoenix, Leslie chatted with another family member and mentioned that he and Janice were on their way to try out the Canyon Ranch Resort for the first time. John T., a client of mine, overheard the conversation and jumped in to insist that he book an appointment with me there. John was a regular guest where I worked as an intuitive and had seen me several times.

Leslie paused and asked John, "And who are you?"

"Your cousin," he replied even though they hadn't seen each other for almost thirty years.

At the ranch, Leslie bumped into me as I exited a lecture. He noticed my name tag and introduced himself, mentioning what a coincidence that we met, as his cousin, John, had just recommended me a few days before. In his mind, our meet up was an accident, as he didn't consciously seek me out. I laughed and said, "Accident ... or synchronicity?"

On the last day of his stay, Leslie decided that if I had an opening, he'd give it a try since we shared a name. Later that day, he sat across from me and professed a healthy dose of skepticism about all psychic abilities. He was surprised at the accuracy of the reading, and his curiosity about his own spiritual gifts woke up, especially when I saw a deep-rooted, yet unexplored, intuitive channel within him.

After that day, Leslie read and explored different facets of spirituality. He taught himself how to meditate and even wrote a book to document his mystical beliefs. Over the years, our friendship and our talks evolved from me/teacher, him/student to different esoteric discussions between friends.

After I mentioned my near-death experience to him, at least part of it, his naturally inquisitive nature prompted him to ask more questions. He encouraged me to write about it since public opinion had shifted and there were more books offered on the subject. I hemmed and hawed, finally agreeing to try it. However, I kept putting it off for various excuses—some of them were valid; others were bits of fluff.

Eventually, his persistence won out, and I began to outline the book and work on a rough draft.

A couple of years ago Leslie asked me more questions about my book. I made some excuses such as the fact that I am not a computer adept and, since I typed only eighteen words a minute, the book progressed slowly. In addition, when I remembered my experiences, everything and everyone, the sounds, and visions, I would gently float away and forget to touch the keys—not the best way to get the job done.

He made me an offer: if we talked once a week, he could ask me the questions about the entire experience and my Dragon-Speaking program would transcribe everything we said. These in-depth conversations helped me to write about my journey. Since he studied spirituality for a decade (including most of the NDE books on the market), he knew what questions to ask, down to the smallest details. It was an offer that was hard to refuse.

Until I sat down to write the book, I had never put my NDE in any linear order. Previously, every night as I started to fall asleep, I would remember different parts of my journey Upstairs. I would focus only on a particular scene or two, of my time in the Hall of Records or the various discussions with the light beings. Most of the time, I would focus on my first arrival, the sense of awe I experienced as I felt that all-enveloping feeling of love. Other times, I would recall the time that I looked up and saw the Unmanifest, the Divine, over my head and the intensity of the love and adoration that I felt.

When Leslie Klein asked me questions, I linked them up in a line. Many more details of the journey opened up, such as when I looked in the river and tried to figure out what swam in it, or a description of the meadow with the plethora of birds and flowers.

Leslie often reviewed what I had drafted. His inquiries brought out many more details in my total experience. For example, when I initially described the beings at the large meeting table, I described Ra-u as the man with long brown hair and a beard who sat on my right. That wasn't enough for him, so he asked me simple questions about Ra-u's appearance. What color brown? (Dark.) What color were his eyes? (Charcoal grey but not flinty. Soft like a charcoal grey.) Was his hair wavy or straight? (Wavy.) Did it hang down loose or was it pulled back into a ponytail? (A slightly messy ponytail.) Is it indeed so important for the readers to know if his beard was trimmed or long? (Neatly cut, not a buzzed stubble.)

Yes, it is essential, and, by asking for countless other details about the visual specifics, the philosophical particulars, and the discussions

I had during my NDE, I wrote a much more comprehensive picture of my experiences than in my first draft. The sixteen pages that I wrote initially more than doubled.

Leslie also helped me to write in a language that most people could understand. I learned that not everyone knows what a "herd boss" is, much less what it means to other horses. Nor would they know the powerful effects that its presence would cause in the group's pecking order, pivotal to my experience, when the "herd boss" is hungry.

We employed the same focus for every single "minute" of my journey. By inquiring in the way he did, week after week, he got me to expand on all that I came across.

Every week I sent him what I wrote, and, when I called, he asked me more and more questions. Working with him brought out the vast array of many particulars in my memory. These details were not something I thought to put on paper. I knew what I had seen, and assumed that what I had written depicted the entire experience. Not so. In trying to paint the bigger picture, I condensed the minutiae. Leslie kept my focus on which aspects did the most good and helped me to flesh out my NDE. For that, I am eternally grateful. Because of his range of questions, Leslie Klein contributed to give the world a broader picture of what life is like in what I have to come to call "Upstairs."

He also asked many questions not related to my NDE, but that covered many different aspects of my spiritual lessons and epiphanies that happened after I returned. That Q & A section appears in Chapter 5.

His persistence to uncover a universal understanding of my words brought up an interesting point: semantics. We all have different dictionaries, yet a clear and logical content is critical to understand the book. If I asked 100 people to go to a hardware store and bring me a sky-blue paint, I'm sure that seventy-five of them will pick different colors and none of them would be wrong because there is no one color for sky-blue. If it's hard for everyone to have the same definition of a particular shade, how difficult would it be to communicate accurately about things that are not tangible?

Take the concept of "Self/self." My interpretation somewhat resembles the Eastern philosophy but simpler. The small "self" is our human awareness and wiring, and the capital "Self" is our spiritual consciousness. My belief is we must integrate the two, not allow one to dominate the other.

As tricky as adequately portraying what Heaven, or what I have come to call Upstairs, felt like, depicting how we communicated or traveled around is equally daunting. Nothing I experienced happened in a linear way. Whenever I conversed with anyone, it tended to be telepathic, and all the information was instantly comprehended. A discussion that might take several pages to recount was understood immediately.

Movement is the most difficult to describe. If I chose to walk somewhere, I would experience the journey in flashes, rather than a direct line as we experience here. I felt no movement in my limbs. It seemed as if several slides dropped down between my goal and me. I existed in each slide, yet the travel was fluid and not interrupted by any sense of choppiness. For this reason, I have chosen to write in a direct, non-stop fashion, as if I walked like on earth so that it wouldn't distract from the narration of the experience.

Everyone who has talked or written about their NDEs says that their experiences are indescribable. That is entirely accurate! Instead of calling the beings I met Upstairs "people," I call them "light beings" because I perceived a slightly fluorescent blue sheen emanating from them. They looked like people, earthlings, no odd tubes or extra limbs or eyes. They were not translucent or see-through. Nothing was: but everything had a slight glow to it.

I also do not differentiate between the words *soul* and *immortal soul*. In other words, I do not think there are different levels: the light body I stood in after I "died" was my interpretation of my immortal soul, my full spiritual consciousness devoid of any human particles of Lesley Lupo, save the knowledge and maturity attained during that lifetime.

The book also reflects the concept of reincarnation. I was born and raised Roman Catholic and the belief taught was that we have one life and go to heaven or hell. However, high school and the Moody Blues pulled me towards the Eastern philosophy. I studied Zen Buddhism, Taoism, and Hinduism and enjoyed reading the Bhagavad-Gita, the Tao-Te-Ching, and the Upanishads. I love reincarnation's viewpoint because I wouldn't mind coming back and helping again, which is the Bodhisattva Vow. I don't know if we will ever have irrefutable, scientific evidence to prove one way or the other or, if it even matters. What if some souls come down once or twice and others come down countless times? Why does one thought or interpretation have to apply to everyone?

This near-death experience surprised me with how it mirrored my longings on earth. As I processed my memories, I realized that now I knew why I had always gravitated towards thick oak forests and the sound of babbling brooks. So many of the colors, symbols, and scenes were familiar and favorites on earth, such as my childhood love of encyclopedias.

And what about the other realms? Some people favor crisp, serene glaciers, or sandy beaches. Others love hot, sizzling deserts, rolling meadows, or lush tropical jungles. This attraction may be because that is their heavenly realm. They respond to some very personal, subconscious memories of a sacred place where they return to between lives.

Often, the same question about near-death experiences is asked. Why are there so many stories today? Moreover, why is there so much interest in this subject now? Death is something that has captivated our attention for as long as we had a questioning mind. Many myths and rituals have evolved regarding the end of life, as we know it. Many people are afraid of it: to date, it is entirely unknown. Others turn their backs on dying and ignore it, but few people face their mortality without questions.

When Raymond Moody published his book, he was the lone voice in the wilderness, yet he persevered. The research, which he started, challenged the scientific materialist point of view that when the body dies, nothing exists because the brain generates all consciousness. Yet, the investigation into NDEs validated long-held beliefs for others; case in point, the *delogs* in Tibetan Buddhism. A *delog* is a person who has died, unexpectedly regains consciousness, and tells details of magnificent spiritual domains in which other spiritual beings review the moral and religious teachings of Tibetan Buddhism. These *delogs* become a bridge between the community and the "other side."

During the last few years, however, the Baby Boomers have begun to face their "Third Act," the same people that actively marched in the sixties for civil rights, gay rights, women's rights, and organic food; all the things we take for granted now as a standard way of life.

At the time, many of the Baby Boomers felt that they should live their lives based on the unity of life, in other words, globally; something the Internet finally allowed the world to do. These same people are now facing aging, isolation, and dying in the same way they confronted other challenges: filled with a plethora of questions regarding the death and the afterlife. They aren't going to fade or float away and leave you to ignore this critical transition. We bring the experience of mortality, of heretofore-unknown change, out in the open as suggested by Morrie Schwartz in *Tuesdays with Morrie* by Mitch Albom. There is a reason that book was a bestseller for so long. As ALS hastened his death, Morrie questioned our perceptions of life:

As you grow, you learn more. If you stayed as ignorant as you were at twenty-two, you would always be twenty-two. Aging is not just decay … it's growth. It's more than the negative that you're going to die, it's also the positive that you understand that you're going to die and that you live a better life because of it."

What if near-death experiences are real? Pretend for just a few minutes that all these extraordinary stories and talk about the boundless selfless love and joy are genuine. Think about what difference that realization would inspire in your life, in your stress levels, and in your goals.

I hope that my story will encourage everyone to find their light within, their immortal soul, and that it will aid everyone who seeks the ability to feel what their subconscious intuition always senses and already knows. It helps to remember who we intrinsically are; we are immortal souls playing the role of a human being. You won't find your inner light by thinking; you can experience it only by *being*. Soothe your proverbial monkey mind and listen to the infinite love and light that you already hold within your true Self.

Lesley Joan Lupo
June 5th, 2018

I don't remember hearing any snorts or whinnies. I don't remember smelling the sweat streaming off the newly unsaddled backs or seeing the dust kicked up by the drumming hooves. The only thing I remember was me, my essence, my soul, popping out of my body several seconds before it was caught up in a stampede. I didn't feel my arm caught in the stirrup or sense the impact of the horse's body as he twisted me around and slammed me with his head. I watched myself cry out as I was squished between the other horses' flanks. Nor did I feel anything as my skull smashed into the concrete feed trough before I collapsed, unmoving. The total peace and serenity that I, the observer, felt was a stark contrast to my screaming human form. I wondered if everyone disconnected like this before they died.

As the dust settled, I looked down at the empty, crumpled shell. I knew I would never get up again. The whole event only lasted about thirty seconds.

PART ONE: MY STORY

"Death is not extinguishing the light; it is putting out the lamp because the dawn has come."

~ *RABINDRANATH TAGORE*

Chapter One

The Doorway

The thirteenth of March 1988 started as a typical day at the Tanque Verde Guest Ranch. My husband, Bob Cote, owned the ranch, so, as VP of Operations, I jumped into any department that needed help. March was always one of our busiest months. That day one of the cowboys had called in sick, so I worked with the horseback riding program. I brought over unsaddled horses, helped guests to mount up, and taught necessary skills to beginners.

After the rides returned, the cowboys would help guests to dismount in the loading arena. At the end of the day, we led the horses into a small inner pen to be unsaddled and brushed. After that, we released them into the main corral that held the feed barn. Some horses stood around wearing feedbags for an extra

1

portion of grain; others had their saddle sores doctored or their shoes checked.

About eighty horses were already unsaddled and on their version of cloud nine: enough bales of fresh alfalfa hay put out to feed one hundred and twenty horses. They could eat without the inescapable disputes that occur when the entire herd finally arrived. Once that happened, the unbendable "pecking order politics" would reestablish itself.

Horses within a large herd are predictable: they bump into each other, ignore their neighbors, flick flies for each other, or fight to maintain their recognized hierarchy. The chain of command begins with the meanest, surliest, stoutest horse taking on all others for the title of "herd boss." Another dozen or so horses just under the boss will buddy up, like lieutenants, and treat the others as if they, too, were in command, although they avoid any confrontation with the boss. Then another group of buddies will form another group under the lieutenants, and so on until all the horses know their place. These groupings also rule who eats first. Since the cowboys unsaddle the nearest horse without regard for its position within the herd, the horses must scrap it out every day to make sure the top horses, i.e., the herd boss and the lieutenants, get most of the food.

When each horse is finally let loose, he bolts down to the hay barn. Every horse wants to *get there first*. When they reach the feed bins, they push and shoulder their way in between the others as if there is a "best spot." It does not matter how much fodder we put into the bins or how many hundreds of bales sit in the center of the barn as a backup. After working hard all day, their innate fear of starvation stirs up their competition for food.

On that day, we brought in the next group to unsaddle. I undid the cinches and removed the bridles. The cowboys tossed the saddles up on their pegs and let them run out to eat. One horse knew how to untie any knot and open a closed gate, so he earned the name Houdini. True to his name, as I reached to loosen his cinch, he nudged back the lock on the gate, slipped out of the pen, and ran towards the hay barn. I jumped forward to close the gate, but another horse snuck through and followed him.

I glanced at the clock. It was 2:50 pm Our last two rides were due to return in ten minutes. The more hungry horses that surrounded the barn, the more difficult it would be to catch the escapees. The cowboys had started at 4:30 am so everyone wanted to finish up. I volunteered to go down to the barn to get them before the final groups returned.

I grabbed a couple of halters and walked through the loading pen to the feed barn. It was essential to bring the horses back before they hurt themselves or wrecked the saddles. The animals all crowded in next to each other. I spun the halter ropes in tight circles to keep the loose horses that waited for their place in line from pushing me aside. What luck! The two saddled horses stood side by side and munched away. With their heads deep in the trough, they were blissfully unaware that I had arrived to bring them back. Either that or they chose to ignore me.

A wall of jam-packed rumps with swishing tails faced me. There were no spaces between the horses; I would have to push and shove my way up to their heads. Even though I clucked my tongue and poked their sides, they stood their ground, afraid to lose their place at the trough. I turned around and tried to force myself in backward by grabbing the stirrups and pushing my arms forward. I finally managed to wiggle my way in as far as the cinches.

Suddenly, my conscious awareness, my soul, popped out and stood ten feet away. "I" watched "me" continue to squirm between the horses. I did not feel any movement. I was here, in my body, one moment and suddenly over there. I watched the horses and my body as it continued to twist and turn between the tightly packed animals as if I was someone else. Shocked, all I could think was, *Wha...?*

I didn't have the time to finish the thought because within a split second, somewhere close by, a horse screamed in fright and instantly, en masse, they all bolted. The sheer power of one 1,200 lb. animal is formidable: multiply that by seven to encounter a deadly force.

The scene I now witnessed happened in slow motion. As the horses scattered, they bumped into me. I spun around and my right arm slipped into the stirrup. Hung up on the saddle, I was unable to free myself. The horses shouldered me and kicked at my legs; the saddled horse felt my body and reacted with terror. He had to get away and could not if he was burdened by dead weight. He dragged me along for a foot or two, then swung his head and slammed it against me.

Because I left my body, I did not feel the crush as the horses bounced me around, even though I watched myself scream in pain. My head crashed into the concrete corner, my arm slid out of the stirrup, and my body hit the ground like a sack of stones. Remarkably, peace flooded through me the entire time I observed the drama. The circle of life completed itself, and there was a sense of normalcy to the whole event. This scene was the way it was meant to be: perfect!

Several horses ran around my battered body while I, my immortal soul, my identity, observed it all. As I gazed down at my crumpled empty shell, I knew that I was dead. I would not be getting up again. It was permanent: I knew it through and through. Yet I giggled as I looked around and thought, *This is it? This is what everyone's so afraid of? I'm still here and I'm still thinking!*

It appeared that I observed everything from a slightly higher perspective. Looking down, I saw that I was floating. With zero gravitational pull, I hovered a few inches above the ground.

I wondered what I looked like, what was left of "Lesley Cote" and looked down at myself. Was I a ghost? My hands looked the same, except they were dazzling. A thin fluorescent-blue mist streamed off them. My jeans and boots, dirt and all, mimicked the same light. I was not see-through, but I was not quite stable either.

I was free! All physical constraints vanished. Previously unaware of how tight and squished one feels inside the human form, I felt fresh and completely unrestricted, as if I had peeled off a head-to-toe body girdle that was four sizes too small. Every cell separated into buzzing particles, and a crisp, sweet breeze blew through. With no aches and pains, I felt completely invigorated and more alive than ever before. Somehow, I balanced this new, crackling vitality with an abundant sense of tranquility. Harmony flowed through from my soul and cultivated a sense of completeness, of oneness with the world around me.

My perceptions intensified. I could hear everything. The horses nickered as they stirred around the feeders and crunched the alfalfa as they chewed. Birds twittered and clacked their beaks. Lizards scratched and scurried through the woven mesquite-branch fence. Every sound magnified as if a thick cotton batting fell off my ears. Instead of dissonant sounds, they all blended into a mellifluous symphony.

In contrast to my ordinarily small, limited field of sight, my peripheral vision widened to encompass the entire corral and barn. Everything was in crisp focus, not blurry. I admired how my perception instantly processed all the new and far-ranging data without any sensory overload.

I did not change into an oblivious ball of light or a particle in a luminous river—or even another person. I was still me, Lesley Cote, but very much alive and as light as a feather. All physical boundaries dropped, and I became breath itself; breath with consciousness. Cosmic breath.

As I relished my newfound buoyancy, Don O. returned from the desert with the fast ride and leaned over to open the lower gate across the corral. The last groups of guests had come back. Bill M. led his group up right behind him. Nostalgia swept through me. I knew what would happen next.

Don moved aside to let the riders enter and closed the latch as I had done so many times before. As he turned to lead the people up to the barn, they all noticed my body face down in the manure. He raced over as he shouted for help from the other cowboys who still were unsaddling. The guests rode over as everyone converged at my body.

One of the guests jumped off his horse and ran over to my body. He turned me over, cleared my breathing passages, and started CPR. Drawn to the event, and without realizing how, I moved over to watch. They gathered around my body in a circle as another guest knelt to help the man do CPR. He pushed on my body and counted aloud as the first man desperately tried to ignite some spark of life in me. Two women stood nearby and held hands as they wept. Others helplessly stood in silence. Every so often, the guest who blew into my lungs checked his watch.

Every breath the people took, the swoosh of their pulsing heartbeats; every whisper they uttered to each other was amplified. I stood lightly on the ground right there, right next to the people who struggled to save my life. I shouted that I felt great and to leave me alone. But no matter how much I tried, no one heard me.

As the cowboy ran to the main ranch house, the stable all around me began to change. The barn, the horses, the people, and the fences all began to fade away into an intensely bright fog. I wanted to linger, to stay where I was and see them all: the cowboys and the guests, the horses, even the manure on which my body lay. A surge of vulnerability passed through me as I watched it fade away.

An endless river of shimmery particles streamed past like a breeze and whooshed around me. I did not move, yet everything around me started to shift and change. Triangular patches of intense blue-white light hovered around me so that nothing bumped or jostled me. These splashes of energy appeared to be conscious, yet I could not recognize what, or who, they were. I felt the separation from the ranch increase as another world developed. I expanded again, lighter than before. A soft crackling buzzed around me, reminding me of the whooshing sounds that I had heard when I saw the Aurora Borealis in Canada.

As my world in Tucson gradually grew dimmer, another realm slowly emerged. Faint outlines of a thickly wooded forest, impenetrable and still, slowly took form. Large oak trees with thick branches stood fully leafed out with ferns clustered at their trunks. Bright green velvety moss partially covered the trunks and roots. Small-multicolored star-shaped flowers carpeted the forest floor. Their unfamiliar scent wafted over, pungent and intoxicating. As this new world came more into view, selfless love covered me and filled me with the purest and most intense sensation of indescribable joy.

Behind me, a large creek about twenty-five feet wide noisily bubbled and splashed over a bed of mottled brown rocks. Off to the left, the trees thinned, and a hollow appeared. The transition from the earth plane to this place—whatever it was—happened so seamlessly that I wondered if this realm had always surrounded my life in Tucson but on another level of energy that existed beyond the human scope of perception and comprehension.

In spite of the thickness of the forest, there were no shadows underneath the foliage. No sunbeams broke through the canopy. I could not discern any particular light source. On the contrary, each twig and leaf, each flower and rock glowed with iridescence, seeming to be lit from within. The entire forest shimmered like sunlight on water. Radiance shone from every plant, tree, rock, and flower, which revealed vivid colors that I had never seen before. A life force flowed through the greenery, and I could see it. The forest manifested itself and danced before me. It all seemed familiar somehow, a dance that I had taken part in many times before.

Quite unintentionally, one recurring thought ran through my mind: *I have to remember this. I have to remember it all.* I reached out to touch a bush right next to me; the wide green leaves were bright and slightly translucent. They glistened yet were dry to the touch. It resembled a hologram, however denser.

A faint rhythmic tune pulsed just beyond my hearing. I wondered if it came from somewhere in the distance. I began to move as things snapped into place around me. Moreover, in spite of the fact that my mind was still alert, I felt much groggier than I did after the accident.

As I moved around, selfless love hung around me like fabric, a veil of spun sugar, sticky and sweet. Even though it felt palpable, it permeated me like energy: I soaked it up from my head to my toes and embodied the essence that saturated all around me.

I knew I was in Heaven or what I would come to call Upstairs. I, or some part of me—at that point I had no idea how to define myself—existed beyond my body on earth. I was still mindful of me, my mind, and that I was dead. That knowledge never left me as I looked around. I felt more at peace than ever before.

I knew this was real. Never once did I feel stupefied. It was not a dream; instead, I was in a heightened sense of an authentic reality. It was so ultra-real that for the first of many times, a sentence popped into my mind: *This is real: earth is the dream.*

I adjusted to the crisp, cleansing energy fields of the heavenly dimension and discovered something absent within me: all negative emotions. The fight or flight reactions that unconsciously formulated part of my human psyche—and all the deleterious reactions that were hard-wired into that system—were gloriously absent. No negative emotions registered in me: no fear, no pain, no anger, no anxiety, and no worries. Even though I was woozy, I did not feel judged or any sense of competition. I did not want to control what surrounded me; nor did I feel the need to "earn" the selfless love that flowed around me. I was lovable and it was infinite; I knew there would never be an end to this.

Time—that physical sense of seconds as they tick by like little soldiers on a march that drained away my future—did not exist, at least as I knew it before. A circular energy kept everything eternally present: Timeless. Nothing could age here.

Even the concept of space, of distance, a "here and there" was different. I encountered one consciousness that connected every particle to the whole. My distant earth-mind seemed like a ticker-tape machine, spewing things out in little lines. Here, Upstairs, all information, all movements absorbed into me instantly. My mind's ability to process all the data simultaneously astonished me.

I basked in the freedom from any worries or fears and trusted in the knowledge that it was permanent. Selfless love was the way it had always been: "I am Loved: I Love: I am Love." As simple as strolling in the sunlight.

My curiosity stirred. I wondered what I looked like and held up my hands. My skin was young and dewy fresh. A few coin-sized bright-gold freckles sprinkled over my hands and arms. There were no adornments, no nail polish, and no jewelry. The blue aura that I could see around me on earth gleamed stronger now, and I could see that it hovered around my edges. Was it a mist? No, fogs are constructed of water particles; this streaming color looked luminous, like a steady glow. I thought it must be a way for energy to solidify, to become manifest. Was this a gathering of particles to keep me present? Could I reverse my flow and stream off into light eternal?

I checked myself out first. I was still in a female form and wore a long, silky ultramarine blue dress. Exquisite gilded flowers, leaves, and sparkly beads covered a shawl collar. A golden woven belt circled my waist and stretched when I tugged it. The capped sleeves had the same floral design on its edge. I reached up and touched my face. My chin was slightly pointy. My hair felt short; large loose curls stopped at my jawline. Oh no, I thought, I love long hair. Why do I have short hair?

Splashing water in the nearby stream called to me. I spotted a narrow trail and moved along. My intentions seemed enough to nudge me along. The tips of emerald green ferns hung down into the water. Everything sparkled. Purple, pink, and yellow wildflower spikes shot up next to the knotty fronds. Birds chirped as they flew around the forest. Silver and gold shapes flashed in the water though I could not tell if they were fish.

I turned back toward the forest. On my left, in a little glen, a table stood upon a deep slate-grey dais. Twelve mahogany chairs encircled it. Many people became visible around the table and regarded me with quiet anticipation. They looked like people, yet unlike them, so I thought of them as light beings. They had that same fluorescent blue light shimmering around them.

Five women and six men stood in twos and threes. Everyone smiled and waited for me to come over. I noticed a narrow path towards the table. On the other hand, did it just appear? I could not tell. Images of the table and people popped up as my thoughts somehow moved me over. Was I always there? Some dreamy veil kept familiarity and recognition (and comprehension) at bay.

The deep lapis lazuli oval table had flecks of gold, which glinted across the reflective surface. The edge was rough and hand-formed. In the center of the table was a three-foot area of wavy lines that flowed straight up, like a heat distortion on the road on a sizzling day.

A dozen sleek chairs circled the table. Beautiful carvings covered the high backs of solid wood; each one displayed a different symbol, intricately made from circles and triangles in the midst of flowers and vines, yet I could not read them.

Recognition reflected in the light beings' eyes as if we had known each other for eons. The nurturing that sparkled from their eyes and smiles filled me with wonder. Waves of love caught me up. Voices welcomed me back. I could have drifted in the warm breeze forever and a day. As the group moved to sit, I went towards a particular place—my seat; somehow I knew it.

Bewildered, as the others sat down, I hesitated behind my chair and gripped the back. I could not budge. These light beings hailed me as if I had just returned home after a long journey. Greetings sounded yet no lips moved nor could I tell which sound came from which being. I heard them through me; their voices echoed inside my head. Was this telepathy?

I paused, unsure of what to say. Instead of the selfless love that poured through me seconds before, a spark of unexplainable sorrow flashed through me; pain coupled with a sense of failure. Then it was gone like a snowflake on a sunny day. How could I feel that emotion here? It puzzled me.

Still woozy and unsure of what might come next, I clung to the back of the chair while cheerful voices continued, "Welcome back ... happy to see you..." No one from my family who passed before was there. However, a couple of the light beings looked familiar—especially a woman who sat to my right. Blue Lady! She was the one who visited me when I was a child. She wore the same cobalt long-sleeved dress and her jet black eyes shone like glass. Intricate gold and silver embroidery covered the neckline and cuffs. Finally, a swell of memories began to play out in my mind's eye. She smiled as I contemplated their effect on my childhood.

Die happily and look forward to taking up a new and better form.
Like the sun, only when you set in the west can you rise in the east.

~ Rumi

Chapter Two
Witness to Spirit

—————⊃●⊂—————

My parents lived in the apartment beneath my father's family
in Chicago at the time of my birth. By the time I was four
years old, I was allowed to climb the stairs to visit my Great
Grandmother, Seraphina di Benedetto, my Nonna, anytime I wanted.
Her English was at the same level as my Sicilian—in other words, except for the words, I love you, *t'amu*, it was non-existent. Even so, it
did not hinder our playtime or communication.

I always cuddled in her lap as she sang Sicilian children's songs. She
touched my nose or pinched my cheeks in rhythm with the music as
she gently rocked me back and forth. My earliest memory of meeting
a light being occurred in the middle of a baking day with Nonna and
Grammy Josephine, or Jo, her daughter. Grammy Jo baked cookies fla-
vored with ingredients that differed from my Mom's traditional sugar or
chocolate chip cookies. We pounded combinations of anise, pistachios,

or figs into sweet fillings. My job was to mix the ingredients. As a reward, I licked the lemon icing off the spoons before we washed them.

I leaned toward Nonna's lap as we waited for the cookies to bake and she began to sing. She touched my nose as she sang and then used her finger like a conductor's baton to keep rhythm with the song. Suddenly, she looked over my shoulder and included someone else in her performance. I peeked behind. A tall woman wearing a cobalt blue dress stood behind me. She smiled as she watched Nonna. Her head almost touched the ceiling. Her skin was burnished bronze, and her black eyes sparkled. One thick black braid fell over her left shoulder to her waist.

She glanced down and looked into my eyes, smiling. I had never seen her before, but Nonna continued to sing, so I grinned back and turned to listen. As Nonna continued to keep rhythm while she sang, she pointed to the lady or sometimes me. However, when the timer dinged, and we stood up to go into the kitchen, the woman had disappeared.

Later that year I had another visit from her at my Grandmother Ruth's house. An avid gardener all summer long, my mother's mother maintained a large flower garden on one side of her yard. I loved all the colors and aromas of the different varieties; snapdragons, stock and pansies mixed in with various bulbs like hyacinth and daffodils. Majestic peonies towered over rows of lily-of-the-valley. I glued myself to her side whenever she headed out to weed, plant, or trim. Today was a planting day, and we had developed a particular strategy: my grandmother would dig the hole and mix in her fertilizer recipe after which I would tenderly remove the plant and pop it into the soil. She explained how a plant's roots could be shocked when they were transplanted, hence her special fertilizer. All day long, I talked to each flower to tell it exactly what we planned to do so it would not be upset. I figured my pep talks helped.

As I transplanted some yellow and blue pansies, several of them changed. The flowers flashed as if lit from within and the bright faces turned towards me as if they listened. Others further away fluttered in the breeze, but these blossoms became super-alive.

A deep blue hem decorated with sparkly gold and silver embroidery appeared in the middle of the flowers, and when I looked up, the lady who visited me before stood there. She towered over me, all the while smiling and radiating light.

"Hi! What's your name?" She did not speak to me, but she nodded and reached towards the flowers I held up to show her. Soft music filled the air. I felt peaceful and loved, delighted and excited all at the same time.

I repeated the question. The blue lady nodded again but still didn't answer. My grandmother was accustomed to my conversing with the plants, but, when she looked over, she saw me staring up at the sky as I talked.

"Who are you talking to?" she asked.

"This lady."

"What lady?"

"This lady with the blue dress." I pointed straight at her. "She's my friend."

"No, Lesley, there's no one there."

"Yes, there is! Right here, Grammy." I pointed again.

My grandmother shook her head. She stood up, took me by the hand, and hurried towards the house. I could tell she was upset, but I did not know why. What did I do wrong? I looked back as we rushed away; the lady waved goodbye. I waved back and decided to name her Blue Lady, but I was puzzled. Nonna seemed to know the woman, she sang to her. However, Grammy Ruth did not see her. She even said the lady wasn't there.

Grammy lifted me onto the table and went to the refrigerator. She handed me a glass of lemonade and got a wet washrag from the sink. She wiped my forehead and the back of my neck.

"Are you tired honey?"

"No, Grammy, but can we go back to the garden?"

"No, not today."

"But my friend is still there!"

"No, Lesley, there's no one there. She's gone home."

I did not argue. I could not understand why my grandmother said that. Grammy Ruth never asked me any more questions about my friend, but, after that, she watched me more carefully when I talked with the flowers. After that, on the gardening days, I had to wear a sun hat.

Soon I started primary school. I did not see these light beings often, but, when one appeared, if I talked to them, an endless supply of classmates and siblings teased me. I soon realized that no one else could see them. That puzzled me and frightened me, both at the same time. Why had no one else noticed them? Whenever they appeared, the gentle, comforting love that came from them soothed me. Eventually, when these kind beings came into view, I learned to keep my mouth shut and smile—unless I was alone with them. Then I felt such joy that I spun around in circles and danced. At other times, I sat down with them and told them everything I had done that day.

They did not appear out of thin air. My surroundings would start to fade a bit. Sounds similar to faint glass chimes sprinkled random notes around the room. Other times, gentle breezes came through the room and tugged at me. Then they came into view, for a split second or up to several minutes. Often they appeared to be distant; at other times, they stood right next to me.

By the grace of a cheerful and tolerant housekeeper, I could read, print, and write cursive before I began first grade. It was no surprise that my school lessons bored me. During the first writing lesson, the teacher illustrated the capital "A" and the small "a" on the blackboard. Instead of following her instructions, I wrote a letter in cursive to my mother and told her how much I hated school.

The bell rang for recess. The teacher told us to turn in our lesson as we walked to the playground. I froze. I thought we would be bringing the papers home. I looked at the floor as, row by row, kids filed past her and placed their lessons on her desk. When I put my paper on the pile, she looked at it, then me, and asked me to stand by her side.

As the class ran outside to play, the teacher took me into the principal's office. Instead of getting in trouble for not doing the assignment, Sister Mary Rosalina set up some individual tests for me. They discovered that I had an eighth-grade reading level. From then on, whenever the curriculum was reading or writing, I got a pass to spend free time in the library along with two other gifted children. It was there I found my first encyclopedia. This sparked a lifelong thirst for knowledge. Not only was each volume packed with lots of information, but, throughout each article, bold text referred to another entry of related facts in another book. I spent a lot of time reading back and forth between books piled on the table. Time flew by unnoticed.

One Thanksgiving our house filled to bursting point with our extended family. We all sat around various tables to share in the feast that took two days to prepare. Turkey, stuffing, homemade cheese ravioli, several different vegetables, potatoes (mashed or baked), candied sweet potatoes and homemade cranberry sauce spread out on top of our kitchen breakfast table.

After cleaning my plate, I wanted seconds and went to get more. When I returned, there, on one of the living room couches, sat another light being: a man with short bright-white hair and wearing a long crimson shirt over ivory pants. French doors divided the living room from the dining room, and I thought they were closed, so I put my plate down on the table and spun around as I chatted. All the sounds of the family in the next room faded away.

The door had not closed completely. Someone heard me talking and opened both doors fully. There I stood, caught up in an animated monolog complete with gestures. My entire family watched. After a few minutes, my theatrics made them chuckle, and then roar.

The sound of their laughter stopped me in my tracks. I spun around, shocked to see everyone watching me. Embarrassed, I ran upstairs to my room. A few minutes later, my Aunt Jo came up with a piece of pie and a hug. She told me not to worry and asked me if I had been playing *The King and I*, which everyone knew was my favorite movie. Even though I would not answer, she convinced me to go back downstairs. After a couple of jokes, they all forgot about it and moved to the TV room for the football games.

But I didn't forget. I was upset that I did not notice the open doors. That light being could see them for he looked in that direction. How could that happen? Why not warn me? I always felt happiness and love when the light beings visited. I thought they were my friends and would have alerted me that we were not alone.

Later that night, I rearranged stuff in my junk drawer. As I pulled out my flashlight for under my bedspread reading, I saw Blue Lady in the corner. I was still upset so I picked up a book and refused to look in her direction. Because of the love and peace they all radiated, I had decided these light beings must be angels. Ghosts sounded too scary, and devils seemed evil, but now I was not sure. Would angels abandon me like that?

Initially, I ignored her, but she stayed put. Out of the corner of my eye, I could see her waiting. I finally asked her why she let me be embarrassed like that. I wanted to yell, but it was way past my bedtime. That was the first and only time I heard any of the light beings speak. I did not listen to her with my ears; I heard her voice inside my head.

She explained that even though I was able to see them, not everyone else could. When I did see them, my awareness of my surroundings became a little fainter. That is why I did not notice when the doors opened and the laughter started.

Blue Lady said, "We weren't abandoning you; no one could block that experience. Your family was not trying to hurt you; they did not see what you saw nor did they understand it. Sometimes we misunderstand what people mean when they say or do things. They thought you were play-acting as you twirled around and found it enjoyable so they were laughing at a performance, not at you."

I still felt a bit confused, but the way she smiled and laughed made everything go back to being all right.

A few weeks later, my mom and I got in the car to go shopping. She had planned to bake a cake with chocolate buttercream frosting but realized she missed two ingredients. As we drove away, in a flash my reality changed. Instead of sitting in the front seat next to my mom, my view, my entire perspective, left the car and floated out through the windshield. I was shocked as the car dropped away and my sight raced straight up the street. I could not cry out. My stomach tightened. Parked cars, trees, and pedestrians whizzed by as I fast forwarded two blocks ahead and wrenched to my right for another block. At that point, a white convertible raced out of a parking lot right in front of me and plowed into the rear tail light of a red four-door car.

Just as quickly, I felt a tug inside my body. My stomach turned as I helplessly endured being pulled back to sit right next to my mom. My head throbbed, and the dashboard spun as I struggled to catch my breath. Mom still talked about the recipe as if nothing different happened when I found my voice and shouted, "Watch out!"

"What?" my mom gasped.

"A car crash!"

"Where?" Her voice rose an octave.

"A red car hit by a white car."

"What? Stop it; there aren't red cars here, Lesley!"

"But Mom, I saw it."

She finally got cross. "Lesley! There aren't any red cars here. Don't scare me like that!"

We drove two more blocks and turned right. Directly in front of us was a red car. I was so startled to see it that I gasped. Mom quickly glanced at me as we drove behind it. Almost as if on cue, as we continued down one more block, a white convertible raced out of a parking lot, cut us off, and rammed the back of the red car.

Several pedestrians ran over to check on the drivers. Angry voices bellowed as they got out of their cars to survey the damage. Mom looked at me. She leaned over and affectionately tousled my hair as we waited. I fought back the tears and looked down at the floor of the car.

Shaking, I could not believe what just happened—the same cars, the same accident, the same everything. No, I kept thinking, no, it cannot be true. I didn't do it; I did not.

One of the men took charge and waved us through. My mother never mentioned the accident again, and for that, I was thankful. Convinced that I caused it, I was grateful no one was hurt. For the next few weeks, I only looked down at the ground. I did not want to see anything or anyone from what I called the "middle place." I did not realize it then, but that was the first time I shut off my intuition.

We are not human beings having a spiritual experience.
We are spiritual beings having a human experience.

~ *Pierre Teilhard de Chardin*

Chapter Three
Awakening

———————

And now I stood in a breathtaking forest. Complete peace surrounded me, and acceptance emanated from the eleven light beings. Even so, wobbly and unsure of what to do, I held on to the chair. Blue Lady was there. Meena was her name; suddenly I knew it. The recognition surprised me, and I almost laughed.

On Meena's right sat a slender woman with short, glistening black spiky hair and vivid amber eyes. Another name, Sala, came into my mind. I was not sure if I remembered her name or whether I heard it telepathically. She wore a dark teal-blue tunic of felted wool. Random swirls of yellow, pale green and light blue ran throughout the fabric. She wore a matching thick, fuzzy headband. The other light beings smiled and waited for me to act. At this point, no one spoke.

I let go of the chair and sat down even though I did not know what to do. The river splashed behind me. I sat with all eyes on me, the center of attention. A couple of voices spoke again and welcomed me back with words of encouragement, yet I was unsure of what to say.

I could only see the people next to me. The central wavy lines on the table blocked a clear picture of the far side. Ancient and immeasurable wisdom emanated from them as they watched me. Immense waves of selfless love washed over me as I glanced from face to face.

A man with a trim brown beard and long wavy hair pulled back into a loose ponytail sat at my right. Stray hairs stuck out which gave him a rumpled look. His dark gray eyes crinkled when he smiled. The name Ra-u came to mind. He wore an ultraviolet, loose-fitting, collarless shirt. The simple thorn embroidery pattern that covered his collar and cuffs was the same color purple as his shirt. His pants, on the other hand, were burnt-orange and odd looking because the colors clashed. Everyone at the table wore such beautiful, harmonious clothing. I wondered why he did not wear indigo or blue pants or even white. Why choose such incompatible shades if he had access to the entire range of colors available in the universe?

Another man with short, almost fluorescent white hair was on his right. I recognized him from my faux pas during Thanksgiving dinner. I also saw him a few other times when I was a child. His pale blue eyes spoke volumes of peace and love. He wore a bright red tunic with star-like lights around his neckline that sparkled to the point of blurring the edges: something I did not see when he was sitting in my living room. The name Teemo popped into my mind.

Another woman with deep ebony skin and short black hair sat next to him. Chama came to mind. Her deep purple top looked as if it was hand cut from a stretchy fabric. There was a hole just under the collar, which tapered off leaving her left shoulder uncovered. A staff leaned on the table next to her, its top covered by multi-colored shells and crystals woven together with colorful threads.

Finally, Meena clapped her hands. Everyone quieted down as she spoke to me. "This must seem confusing."

I tried to talk, but my mouth mumbled like it was frozen. Somehow, my message went out telepathically. "I'm shaky. When will it pass?"

"That depends on you," Meena said. "You've been in an accident, and, even though your connection to earth has broken, you're not here either. To be in one place completely, you must make a decision."

Stunned, I was amazed at how swiftly I understood. As soon as Meena formulated the first word, the entire message popped into my mind and, just as quickly, I completely understood.

"How did I get here?" I had no memory of the accident.

Meena smiled as she pointed towards the center of the table. The wavy lines formed a three-foot sphere, and the scene of my accident appeared inside. Everyone watched the energy ball as a 3-D movie began. The hay barn at Tanque Verde Ranch came into view. I do not know how it happened. I did not see any buttons pushed or any switches flipped.

The reenactment appeared so real that I wondered if I could reach out and touch the horses. Lesley Cote walked down to the hay barn, Stetson hat firmly in place with spurs jingling. The halter ropes spun as I neared the herd. Then I turned and tried to wiggle in between the two saddled horses.

As the story unfolded, memories resurfaced, and I felt waves of nostalgia. This movie showed the accident from a bird's eye perspective so I could see the entire corral that now included the saddling area.

After I left, the cowboys continued their work unsaddling the horses. As usual, they grabbed the closest horse. It happened to be the herd boss named Montana. He was a big, brash, chestnut quarter horse with four white stockings and a white blaze down his face. The cowboys pulled his saddle and turned him out just as I turned around to push my way between the two horses. Montana trotted down to the feed bins. He was just as afraid of missing a meal as any of the other horses.

Belligerently, he neighed and laid his ears flat back before he took a quick nip at the closest rump. That tiny bite was enough to send the others into a panic; several horses on either side of him bolted which opened up a place at the feed box.

I watched as the horses wheeled around and turned. I spun, catching myself on the stirrup. I watched the horse slam me with a head bump and smash me against the corner of the feed box. Then my body dropped like a stone and lay utterly still.

In the sphere, I did not see my soul next to my body. When the scene faded, the energy did not completely disappear. The wavy lines straightened out and stayed put.

Silence prevailed. Unspoken support intensified which sent an amplified sense of selfless love to encircle me. My overriding thought was how safe I felt, how protected. I closed my eyes as I tried to elicit an emotion. Watching myself die was solemn, but I did not feel tragic or sad. It was what it was, a routine and simple part of life. I experienced the same serenity that I encountered on earth when I witnessed my death.

I opened my eyes, and Meena suggested that we continue to look at my history. She looked back at the lines, which formed a sphere again, and different scenes of my life on earth displayed randomly in no chronological order. The apartment building in Chicago where I had lived as a baby popped up first, then pictures of my siblings. In Santiago, Chile, I leaned out over my balcony and observed people down on the street. Then I was a young child again and back in Oak Park, Illinois, climbing a tree in our backyard. Next, it was my grandparents' home in Menominee, Michigan, then a shot of some scattered sailboats as we raced across Green Bay. Quickly, I was back in Oak Park late at night on my four-poster bed with a flashlight under the covers of my white tufted bedspread as I read past my bedtime. The scene then switched to my apartment in Rabat, Morocco, then the Institut de France in Paris, France, before it bounced back to a party in my dorm at the University of Albuquerque. Overall, about thirty to thirty-five images played out.

The pictures ended. Breezes tossed my hair. Everyone at the table remained quiet. I could hear the river splash behind me. Again all eyes rested on me. I still did not know what to say.

Thankfully, Ra-u spoke up. "Do these help you to remember anything?"

"I remember some of them," I said.

Meena said that I had to make a choice. She explained this was what remained of my soul group. We answered a call to incarnate with the shared goal to help raise awareness. Most of the group agreed and incarnated. The rest stayed behind to continue our work there. I planned to return early with one particular light being from this group. At the age of twenty-one, I had agreed to return with him.

However, right before the crash, my immortal soul balked and decided not to leave. Ra-u added that I loved the earth so much that I decided to stay and continue to help. Nevertheless, since I had not incarnated with a long-term plan, I had to script the rest of my life on the fly. Now I faced a clear-cut choice: to stay Upstairs or choose to go back to Tucson. Both options were available. Ra-u mentioned that my decision would not be an easy one.

"Your decision to stay behind didn't cause any problems," Meena added. "You had the freedom to choose your departure before you went down. Any assistance is beneficial to the overall growth and healing of consciousness. Now you have two children, which you did not initially sign up for, and your decision affects them too. Don't decide now; take your time to think about it."

Children? What children? I did not see any children in those pictures, nor did I remember them. I was still overwhelmed by the ab-
sorption of information in this "instant" format. All the information
instantly appeared in my awareness intact.

Ra-u rose and asked, "Why don't we take a walk? I'll take you to a
cave under a waterfall nearby. It's a place you loved to visit."

With that, Ra-u and I stood up to leave everyone and moved to our
left around the table. I nodded goodbye to everyone as we passed. The
trail stretched deeper into the forest. Before they were out of view,
I turned around to wave. Most at the table waved or touched their
hearts. One did not. He was closer to me now, seated to the left of the
opposite end of the table. I had not seen him because of the energy
sphere. He smiled as he faced the river. He seemed to be entranced by
the rushing water.

Iridescent birds flashed all around the forest. Rainbows reflected in
their feathers as they flew through the branches. We traveled through
the trees on a pounded dirt path. The woodland finally thinned into
an open green meadow that rolled gently towards steep, cloud-cov-
ered mountains. The beaten trail dwindled down to a small footpath.

Ankle-deep lush grass spread out in all directions. Butterflies fluttered around a multitude of bright rainbow flowers; blues, reds, and
yellows grew above the verdant green. Some flowers resembled daisies;
others looked like a single tube. Over to the right and far away there
stood a grove of large trees. Glittering golden buildings rose above
the foliage. We continued to move towards the mountains. Waterfalls
tumbled down from pale speckled cliffs and created the rapid stream
that flowed on our left.

I intuited what happened next before I saw it. With every step I took,
selfless love engulfed me with a new level of intensity. At first, I thought
I had become more open to my surroundings. As the waves continued
to flow through me, I sensed that this selfless love had a point of ori-
gin and that it came from above me. Ra-u did not seem to notice, but
I stopped and looked up.

The sky was not pale and monochromatic; it was multi-colored and
looked as if it had a depth to it. Numerous translucent streaks of ultramarine blues overlapped like a mélange of watercolor washes, reminding me of some apatite specimens. Directly overhead, a central point
of energy emitted love and radiance that defies description. It moved,
but not like the sun traversing the sky. It remained in one spot: fluctu-
ating energy waves poured down upon Ra-u and me. They resembled

water's ripples when a stone drops into it, yet these undulations were being generated by the conscious *something*, or rather ... *someone* which lovingly watched me.

The luminous sphere vibrated so quickly that the edges folded over on themselves and blurred. It radiated visual colors and pulsating energy waves of selfless love. They rhythmically coursed around me and through me as if I were a hologram. The form did not have a hard edge yet was not lifeless. I wanted to remember it all, but I could not think of ways to comprehend the indescribable. It did not fit into any category that I could remember. I struggled to define what I saw and felt. *He* or *She* did not cover the experience, yet I could not look at this heavenly source and say *it*. Ultimately, I resonated with the term, "the Divine."

Above me radiated a living presence that revealed wisdom, compassion, devotion, and a sense of ultimate truth. I knew I stood before the One, the Divine, who displayed the entire splendor and majesty of reality as naturally and effortlessly as I wore my dress. Everything emanated from the center, and I knew everything surrounding me could be changed and reconfigured at will.

If cumulus clouds typically begin at 2,000 feet, the Divine appeared that high. It looked 100 yards across and spherical. Concentric geometric energy waves flowed across the sky and broke into shimmery points of light that made patterns, which resembled mandalas. Vibrating patterns made up of soft, lustrous colors flowed in every direction. The points journeyed away from the center in repetitious arrangements. Other groups of lights seemed to circle the orb. Angels? Distant chanting floated down but in an unusual language. No telepathic understanding came forth. It streamed like a beautiful dance in which this center of sentience, this Divine, manifests things in and throughout all levels of being, of matter, of energy.

Yet the unfolding continued. The Divine knew me; every particle and every quark of me was revealed and laid bare. I tingled with delight. I loved the Divine but what startled me was the level of love I received. I adored the Divine, and the Divine adored me. Adored! I stood thunderstruck in complete awe. Adored by the Divine! The love coursed through me, aligning every single bit of me into accepting this as perfectly reasonable. I did not have to work for it; I deserved it for just being—no action needed. Me: adored for being a collection of energy sparks with a personality.

I had no experience of separation. All the Divine's love was fully present in me, in my every speck and smidgen. I realized I could stretch my boundaries and expanded myself even further out; I could feel our energy patterns unify as we vibrated at the same frequency.

As I regarded the presence above, I could not move. Somehow, I knew I could float up and ultimately merge with that manifestation. I began to lift until only my toes touched but, at that moment, Ra-u, who had stopped a few feet away and quietly watched, put his hands on my shoulders and guided me back to the pathway.

I stared up at the sky again. The designs continuously created new patterns, like a kaleidoscope. I stopped, awe-struck with joy until Ra-u again nudged me onto the path.

I turned to look back one last time and noticed something else. The mottled sky looked as if it was a filmy glass ceiling and, through it, I saw another realm. The top of our world appeared to be the floor of another. It brought to mind a cluster of bubbles—all of them stacked one on top of the other. These realms were transparent enough to see that different patterns faintly moved within the other domain.

I marveled at the multitude of fields of energy above us and asked Ra-u, "What is past our sky? Is this world the final destination for our souls? Can we go to those other ones? What are they? They look like bubbles."

Ra-u smiled as he glanced up. He watched the movements for a moment then replied, "Do you think this is the only place? Many realms make up other dimensions; those are some of them. Some are all color, or all sound. Some are all particles, but all with conscious beings experiencing the infinite multitude of forms. Even if you merge with the Divine, you can come out again if you wish. We go up, turn around, and come back again. The levels are infinite and yet subtle and weightless as they ascend." Then he chuckled, and I laughed with him as if it all made perfect sense to me.

Ra-u put his hand on my back to guide me. Whenever I wandered off in a different direction, I got another nudge.

The land got a little steeper, but we fast-forwarded with no effort. As we approached the mountains, the ground on our right rose to form foothills strewn with boulders. Small shrubs climbed the sides of the foothills until slabs of mottled grey and pink rock rose to the clouds.

The meadow skirted around the bottom of a hill and ended on a cliff's edge. I heard the sound of roaring water. A mist rose and behind it poured a huge waterfall. Several waterfalls cascaded down and merged into the large one that churned and splashed in a sizeable pool. Ra-u said this was where my soul group relaxed and swam.

At the pool's edge, several great clear quartz crystals pushed through the foliage and towered over my head. At the brink of the basin, one unusually wide crystal divided the watercourse into two. One stream ran directly over the cliff and the other ran back towards the forest.

"Wait, come over and see this," Ra-u said.

To our left, a small bridge crossed the stream. We went to the cliff's edge and saw an ocean of the deepest blue stretch out to the vast horizon. The beach looked infinite, too. The sand sparkled and flashed with a blue-white fire like billions of tiny diamonds. Hundreds of muted light brown, sage, and rose-colored tents spread out along the beach. Multi-colored decorations brightened up the fabrics that elegantly draped over the carved wooden posts. Long narrow flags fluttered everywhere; some from the tent poles, but others stood alone. The beauty astounded me.

Substantial pink boulders, which resembled rose quartz, crowded against each other. There were no plants of any kind. Dolphin-like creatures jumped and twirled from the depths and birds flew everywhere. Some light beings moved between tents while others played in the surf or dived in from the boulders.

Surprised by the simplicity, I realized that I missed the flora. The landscape looked a bit austere to me, and I said so to Ra-u. He explained that this was an entirely different place. "There are countless other realms. Our group has visited the beach from time to time, but, when we dwell here, we all prefer the ancient forests and rivers."

Far out on the horizon through the sky, I could see additional levels upon levels of other realms. A veil hung between us, filmy and thin, but a covering nonetheless.

We crossed back over the bridge. At the edge of the pool, Ra-u pointed to another path and said, "If you go around this way, you'll get behind the falls to the cave. It's one of your favorite places to go for solitude. Why don't you go there and rest? When you're ready, go back to our home. See the tall buildings by those treetops over on the left? Go there, and we'll find you. We'll meet with you again when you come back."

We said goodbye. I found the narrow path that twisted through the crystals and rocks. The ferns quivered and moved when I touched them. The flat rocks that edged the pool looked cool and inviting. Rays of sunlight emanated through the crystals and made rainbows on my skin. I ignored an impulse to jump in. The trail continued to an ample space behind the roaring torrent. Before I entered the cave, I turned to look through the cascade. Individual droplets glistened. I reached out and gently trailed my hand through the stream. I saw that my hand cut the stream in two, yet I felt no resistance. The water flowed so quickly that it resembled sunbeams pouring down. I stood there, mesmerized.

I have no idea how long I stood there. Upstairs, with no sense of any linear time or motion, everything occurs at the perfect moment and each moment is vast.

I entered a large cave. It was about forty feet wide, though the slightly curved ceiling was about fifteen feet high at the highest point. The entire cave looked to be hand carved out of pale white marble. Diffuse radiance reflected throughout, generated by the dazzling stone. A flat bench of softly polished silvery marble was on one side of the cave.

Behind me, the waterfall roared. I moved deeper into the cave where two chairs sat, but someone occupied one of them. He had dark brown jaw-length hair, a trim beard, and richly colored dark-grey. Radiant, sparkly, golden-white light blurred all the edges. As soon as this being stood, I knew the name. Jesus waited for me. My heart swelled even further with selfless love.

He smiled and, gesturing towards the bench, said, "I have come to help you. Please lie down and relax. You have worked hard; now it's time to rest. We all appreciate what you have been doing."

He held a white marble container with a silver rim. I sat on the bench and pulled my feet up as I turned to lie down. Pungent sandalwood and rose oil wafted throughout the cave. I closed my eyes and could feel the mixture dabbed on all of my chakra points—including the fainter ones on my wrists and palms, ankles and feet. Jesus smiled all the while; I peeked a few times. He saw me do it and laughed. The moment our eyes met, that wave of sorrow spilled over again. I realized it originated from a deep well of self- criticism.

Jesus shook his head. "Many light beings incarnate to help bring in a new level of forgiveness, like you. While you lived, no matter who hurt you, by accident or by design, you always found a way to forgive them. That is what changes the world. People who learn to forgive truly will make their spiritual growth permanent and be able to work with others for the benefit of all. Moreover, that affects the overall happiness of every one on earth. One idea or person will never create a permanent change for the entire planet. You all must work together while respecting the differences."

Jesus went on to explain that acceptance of differences and true compassion will help permanently to shift consciousness. He continued, "Forgiveness is more than just stifling your anger. Forgiveness can only occur when one fully comprehends the motivation of the others involved. We can forgive them for their wounds, for their lack of mindfulness, for their pain-motivated behavior. They have their lessons to learn. After that, to forgive yourself is the hardest lesson. That is the source of your sorrow now. It came from a sense of being helpless and overwhelmed by witnessing problems that you could not fix.

"You'll make your decision soon. While I am not here to influence you, if you do come back here to stay, you'll continue to be a great aid to those below. If you return, your work will be as helpful as you connect with others like yourself on earth. You must let go of any judgmental thoughts and make this decision with a clear and rested heart."

His eyes radiated immense love and patience. I smiled as I closed my eyes. He playfully plopped one more dollop onto my forehead. Even with the brightness around me, I slipped away. I am not sure if I napped, but, when I opened my eyes, Jesus was gone. I lay still and listened to the splash of the water. Finally, I climbed down from the bench and walked out of the cave, and looked through the wall of water. Splashes glistened like tiny rainbows. I trailed my fingertips in the water one last time.

I felt completely refreshed. I left the pool behind and veered towards my left. A grove of taller trees stood at the end of the meadow. Ra-u and the others would be there.

I did not have a conscious plan but, finally, I was ready to face my choices. In the beginning, in my groggy state, I wanted to stay and had no interest in returning. Ever.

At this point, I still wanted to stay and bathe in infinite selfless love and light, yet another part of me wanted to consider the other option. As I approached, I saw a few miles away yet another group of buildings that looked like a separate town. Further away, another village crested the hill and beyond that, another.

I arrived at the edge of a village. I passed through some scrub trees and entered a park of exquisitely manicured flower gardens. Smaller trees added to the design and were in full flower. Stone pathways bordered the flowers and shrubs. Two substantial buildings rose above the trees from the middle of the garden and stood surrounded by three smaller structures. The circular layout around them resembled mandalas. Scads of other light beings were there. Some strolled along while others sat and visited. Even though no one marked my passage, I did not feel ignored or slighted.

The most prominent building's windows glistened as if wet and made a regular grid of horizontal and vertical panels. Several long and narrow rectangles stood next to a larger one, after which the pattern repeated itself. Gilded beams, covered with painted symbols, ran from ground to roof. Iridescent highlights traversed the windows and reflected the world around me so I could not see into either one. The second had asymmetrical patterns in the glass, random and irregular. It seemed as if it stood a little lop-sided, which gave me the impression of movement; flow.

I chose to go into the first because of the symmetry. I felt grounded when looking at it.

Two great golden doors lay wide open as I approached. Vines, plants, and animals covered the carved edges: some I did not recognize. Long wooden planks with sculpted edges fastened on their sides made up the center of the door. The raised edges ran from top to bottom and covered with occasional bumps. It looked unfinished and caught my attention, so I stopped to study the pattern. Little memories tugged yet again. If I ran my fingers over the edges, would I understand some information? Was I gazing upon a different kind of braille?

I entered through the doorway into a vast room and stopped, astonished at what lay before me. Although it did not appear very significant from the outside, a domed football stadium could have fit inside. Tiles of ivory-colored marble with a tiny burnt sienna matrix made up the floor. Countless wooden drawers, like old dentist cabinets, covered the walls from floor to ceiling. They varied in shape. All had different colored knobs—white and ivory mixed in with soft polished gold, silver, and copper.

I walked over and opened one. A scroll with a thin blue ribbon wrapped around it lay in one of the shallow drawers. I untied the ribbon and unrolled the document. Even though the paper had a toothy texture, it spread out quickly and flattened in my hand. I did not recognize the writing. A deeper drawer held a book. I put it back after I flipped through a few pages and continued into the building. Rolling ladders rested in each corner of the room. Overstuffed velvet chairs in rich jewel-tones stood in groups of twos and threes throughout the center of the chamber, yet all were empty.

Transepts about forty feet across lay on each side and were carbon copies of the main room. I went into the first one on my left and opened another drawer. I pulled out another little book and felt a foggy familiarity with the text. Happiness coursed through me along with pangs of homesickness. I put the book back and returned to the main room.

The ceiling, adorned with carved and painted beams, stood a good thirty feet above my head. Golden-hued landscapes with beautiful Prussian blue frames rested between the corbels. About halfway through the building, I noticed a large circle with an eight-spoke wheel in the ceiling. It was twenty feet wide and opened to the sky. *Okay, so it does not rain here*, I thought.

A sleek ivory Bakelite pedestal stood in the middle of the room and looked out of place in such an elegant Renaissance décor. It had a futuristic look of a 1960s Jetsons cartoon.

As I examined the podium, another brilliant light being, a woman, approached me. She stood twice my height and wore a bright white robe embroidered on the edges with delicate gold beads. A third of the way down, soft purple began to show and, by the time it reached the hem, the color became deep indigo. Pale violet light emanated from her so brightly that it blurred her feet.

Her chocolate brown eyes looked deep into mine, and she smiled as she greeted me. Until now, I perceived everyone's name telepathically. Her name, however, puzzled me. When she introduced herself, I heard only an extended melody. I asked for her name again, and, when she repeated it, all I heard was the same musical sound, soft and beautiful, but still beyond my understanding. It seemed like a group of vowels musically strung together.

I shook my head. She laughed again and said back on earth, her name was Saraswati. She then explained that we were in the Hall of Records, which housed all information, inspiration, and creativity. Never locked, every bit of information was available to anyone who chose to visit, but only if one approached without any trace of ego.

Saraswati asked if I recognized these rooms. I looked around and replied no. She told me that this building was one of my absolute favorite places to visit as I enjoyed researching new information on my breaks. Since I had jumped my contract, I must have sought out storehouses of knowledge on earth: that would be keeping with my level of curiosity.

"Learning here is as festive an activity as relaxation is on earth," she continued. "The color and patterns in the knobs and the shape of the drawers reflect the information stored within. You would take out a scroll or a book, sit down and read it, then put it back and pick out another volume from an entirely different place. It was a never ending stream of knowledge. The whole room continuously grows. As humanity evolves, so do the records. All the new information is updated."

The thought of adding more drawers seemed impossible. I looked around. "How? Every inch is packed. I don't see any space."

"It is all energy, therefore malleable. The wall will shift, and more information adds to the volume already there, or another scroll or book that has space inside."

With this, she laughed, and notes as bright and crisp as glass chimes filled the air. At this point, I realized the information transfer was as before, instantaneous, and it felt in balance.

Saraswati said she came only when called and asked how she could help. I explained that I had a couple of questions, but first, I did not completely understand what she meant by "jumping my contract." In addition, if I have a choice now, then somehow, a part of me decided to come back Upstairs. Why would I do that? And why had I returned at this precise moment?

I must decide if I should return to earth or stay. After my time with Jesus, I understood better what I needed to address. Something had forced me to my tipping point: something I could not remember. A flash of grief shot through me again, but, this time, the message was loud and definite: I did not do enough. That feeling was based on an overwhelming sense of helplessness: the very same emotion from which my lack of self-forgiveness emanated.

Saraswati reached down and touched my forehead. As she did so, a memory popped into my mind's eye. I sat on the brick veranda at Tanque Verde Ranch and read the newspaper. A portrait of three beautiful children caught my eye. My son was five months old, so I felt a maternal tug as I turned to read the story. It turned out to be a piece about a woman who had just escaped from jail. Years ago, she drove up to a hospital and claimed that someone tried to carjack her and subsequently shot her and her children. Caught up in an affair with a married man who, she knew, did not like children, she decided to get rid of them. Afterward, she could try to entice him to leave his wife to marry her. Her lies became apparent as soon as the investigation started.

The story hit me hard. When initially I viewed the photo, I felt my heart open with love for those chubby-cheek smiles. However, as I read the article, my heart chilled, and shock slid down my spine. How could anyone do this? My hands shook as I put down the paper.

Countless people would have adopted the children. Why kill them? As the memory finished, I recognized the voice in my mind, a voice I had not been able to turn off. It began as a whisper in my mind. *If only someone had known; if only someone could have taken away her children. It morphed forcefully into if only I could have kept them safe. I wish I could have prevented it if only, if only, if only …*

Logic had no place in my mind.

The story was a testament to the cruelty that humans will inflict heartlessly on other people, animals, and even plants. I had enough of man's inhumanity to life. Something within me, some form of hope, clicked off and, with that click, my inner light diminished.

"How could a mother murder her children?" I asked. "Rage-filled violence by humans against any living thing is bad enough, but this crime has to be the worst of the worst."

"All normal, healthy humans," Saraswati said, "all compassionate individuals can develop the same sense of shock when they continuously read about any form of abuse. You incarnated to help and to grow in spirit. You hear the voice that calls from your inner divinity to aid others who are suffering. You cannot help every single one. Many loving humans have that same reaction, but, for you, at that moment, it interrupted your ability to feel any hope at all. To live without hope is to plunge into complete despair."

She paused before she continued. "There is a stable arc of moral growth on earth. Keep yourself aware of that fact, too, because often it seems hidden. Don't focus only on the problems that still need to be solved. No one will ever find a lasting sense of happiness until people work together. There are too many people on earth now for one person's actions to affect everyone, whether it is to heal their suffering or to conquer and keep people under permanent control. Empires last shorter now.

"The key now is cooperation. All the tiny acts of kindness combined weigh more than one grand gesture. There is only one way: a unified field of effort to treat all life with dignity, with respect, no matter who they are. This will cause an enduring change. People can make a difference—from his or her home, their workplace, or house of worship. Unity of oneness will bring a state of happiness and that day is coming.

"Inspiration and hope are kept alive by keeping your eyes on the next step, not on the end goal. Now, even as we speak, seeds of divine light and awareness filter throughout the universe and all beings. These seeds cause more and more people to see a unity of purpose. The more that everyone focuses on what we share together, the more we will experience Heaven on earth.

"And jumping your contract is possible for any older being that willingly returns to help. Therefore, as you felt the departure day coming, your immortal soul decided to veer off course and stay. Many, not all, can stay longer than their agreements outline.

"As to why now? The timing was perfect for you to come back." She drew a long and narrow "V" on a paper that materialized on the pedestal. Each point had a differently shaped dot on its end. It looked like a crack in a wall. Was it something to slip past? Completely puzzled, I looked at her. Even though I had no conscious idea what it meant, we smiled together and I accepted this information.

"Everything lined up for you to come here and return with minimal harm, which is why your soul chose to return. If you do go back now, you will help to ground a different type of light. You first went down to ground forgiveness. Now the mission of everyone who incarnates is to bring a higher level of hope. You will find it within yourself first and then teach it."

When Saraswati's message finished, she touched her heart and nodded to me. I knew we were done. I placed my hands in a *namaste*. As I left, I turned to look back one last time at the beautiful building. Meena waited outside the door. She smiled and beckoned me over.

"I think I'm ready to decide." Something in me shifted. I felt a gentle pressure begin to build within.

"Okay, come with me. Some of our group is waiting."

"Is that where we're going?" I indicated the village off in the distance that I had seen when I initially walked up to the buildings.

"No," Meena said, "we live and work around the Hall of Records. That area is for younger souls, and the other village further away is for even younger ones. There are more you cannot see that go the way over to the village of the firstborns. Some Elders live there and guide them and we go there to help, too. You teach there when you are here. If you went there now, you would pass through a hilly area with many different bowl-shaped grassy outdoor theaters. Do you remember them?"

At first, I shook my head, but then a little flash of memory stirred. I pictured a circular green bowl with grassy steps shaped like the Greek outdoor theaters but filled with light beings.

"Smaller circles become occupied by particular souls that regularly send extremely high levels of healing to all the realms," she continued. "After a natural disaster or war, a massive amount of communal pain is generated. That dissonance hangs in what you have come to call the collective unconscious. It looks like a foggy band of negative energy. Tens of thousands of souls assemble in the larger circles to concentrate on sending the highest level of love and inspiration to the afflicted area."

We approached one of the smaller buildings. Beautiful songs re-sounded all around, much louder and more distinct, yet I still did not remember the language. Shiny bluish-white beams ran the length and breadth of the building and held up silvery windows in which the beauty of the garden outside reflected.

We went through an arched entryway about twelve feet tall. A beautiful abstract mosaic of large and small-intertwined spirals covered the entire structure. Light sparkled off the different hues of its blue and green tiles.

To our left, a great room similar to a communal room in a dormitory or office building filled the entire side, with tables and chairs scattered at random. The outside wall had floor-to-ceiling windows, and the ceiling was two stories high.

A few hundred light beings gathered in different groups and talked. Some sat alone and looked as if they were meditating. A few of them waved. Although I did not know them, I waved back.

Meena walked straight down a hallway with a dark grey floor that appeared to be stone but felt soft to the touch. It gave slightly under my steps, and I realized that I had been walking barefoot the whole time. I scrunched my toes on the spongy surface.

Beautiful landscape paintings hung on the mushroom-colored walls and potted plants crowded in the corners. Brightly feathered birds flew in and out. They came closer than before, and I stopped to watch one land on a flower and sing. I steadied myself by leaning on the wall. For the first time since I began my journey Upstairs, I felt a little tired.

We turned down a corridor to the right and passed several closed doors, all of them painted different matte colors of red, green, or blue. Each one displayed a different symbol that I could not read. After passing three more doors, we stopped. Meena opened it, and we walked in.

The room we entered was about 20 x 40 feet in size, and the entire wall on the far side looked dark and wavy like a wall fountain. Throughout the community, many fountains stood near buildings and shrubs. While the sound of splashing water was as universal as the songs and melodies, this fountain flowed silently. Again, I was mindful of my fatigue.

Four of my core group sat around the table; Ra-u, Teemo, and another woman and another man, neither of whom I recognized. The unidentified woman's light brown hair was braided into a headband. Glass hairpins held it in place. Yellow ocher beads dangled from the ends and matched her tawny skin and eyes. She wore a chamois-colored tunic with a wide symmetrical neckline that draped off her shoulders. The edging was a free form cut rather than a neatly turned top. Her monochromatic color palette differed from her startlingly bright white pants. The man wore a similar tunic in deep pine green, which complemented his dark olive skin, black eyes, and buzz-cut black hair. My telepathy seemed to be shutting down; I could not get any sense of their names. I did not ask.

This couple had an interesting relationship with each other. As they held hands, their spirit fields entwined and they lit up the room in a particularly pleasant way. They must have been on the other side of the hologram at the first table, the side I could not see.

Meena and I sat down. Everyone quietly waited. Serenity and a soothing peace ensued as our energy fields joined. Each light being's vibrations harmonized together so that a calm group pattern established itself. It felt like a tremendous spiritual sigh had transpired. This sharing worked on a subtle level. I continued to be amazed at how quickly and thoroughly I followed their messages. Linear processing ceased; all information appeared in my awareness, totally accessible, and I understood.

Ra-u asked about my walk. Images of my experiences with Jesus and Saraswati flashed throughout the group. I informed them that I was almost ready to decide but still had some questions. They all laughed and remarked that I had not changed. I guess I have the same high level of curiosity Upstairs as I do on earth. Their smiles and gentle banter let me know that my decision was as pressure-free as deciding between having a molten chocolate cake or a flourless chocolate tart for dessert.

Initially, I had no interest in leaving. However, after my recovery, I felt more grounded and capable of considering both options. We began by discussing Saraswati's comments regarding "jumping my contract" in more detail. When mentioned to me in the forest, I did not grasp the full effect of that statement. Now stabilized, I approached the decision in a clear-headed way and wanted to hear more details like, why did I go down in the first place?

Meena motioned towards the energy waves once again. The bottom of the large waterfall and pool came into view with about thirty light beings present. We were taking a break from our placement job. Many were in the water swimming while others sat on the large flat crystal and relaxed.

Suddenly a loud cracking sound split the air. An intensely bright ball of blue-white light rippled through whatever opening had formed.

It grew into an angel and stood double my size. The energy was so radiant I could barely distinguish any details. All exchanges were telepathic and in a choppy singsong manner.

The message was clear: a group of volunteers needed to go to earth to intensify an energy shift already underway. Adding older souls would change the thought process from an exclusive, self-centered focus to one that considered global concerns. Many of our group got up and walked towards the Angel. Ten stayed behind to facilitate spiritual support for the twenty that walked over. No one was wet after leaving the water. Others joined our group from different directions until the crowd numbered into the thousands. They sorted themselves out telepathically.

As they walked over to the launching area, many discussed how long they would stay. The Divine mind filled everyone with a buzzy kind of energy. As we entered the building, we noticed that many other light beings had already arrived. We rested in stillness as we awaited our placement and, one by one, we left.

The images changed back into wavy lines as Meena continued. "Your group went over to incarnate in the Great Hall which is that big building next to the Hall of Records. You and another light being agreed to go down as a couple and come back when you were twenty-one by going through a car accident. Because you loved the earth and everything on it—the plants and animals, the mountains and seas, the different cultures and all the people—your immortal soul, your divine consciousness, decided to stay and, at the last moment, turned away from the accident.

"Most stick to their plans and complete their missions. From time to time, an older soul will choose to stay longer than it had initially planned. To pull away from the intended departure takes an immense amount of concentration. Younger souls cannot do this. Usually, at the moment of their death, particular light beings guide them back. They have not developed the inner strength to stabilize themselves as they leave their bodies.

"You must decide if you want to stay or return. If you do go back, do you want to remember this visit? We suggest that you do, but it is not required or automatic. Memories of this experience can add to your resolve, but, at the same time, they can be a burden. To remember everything here will isolate you and, with that knowledge, life will be difficult. It will seem at first that you have a key yet cannot find the lock that it fits."

A surge of intense emotions flashed through me, so I stayed quiet and allowed the group radiance to bring me back into balance. Surrounded by so much support and love, I could not imagine how one could feel alone. I thought these memories would be enough to bring me the solace and inspiration that I would need.

In the center of the table, another energy sphere appeared. Ra-u spoke up. "You didn't sign up to have children. But after you changed your life path, you did, and now you have two."

First, the corral and the hay barn where I died came into view. Next, images of my family and friends began to show up until, for the first time, my children appeared. Brenna was three and Cale was one. Cale stood with his tiny hands covering his face as he cried. To comfort him, Brenna had placed her arms around him, but tears ran down her cheeks too. While I felt an enormous amount of empathetic and protective love, from a cosmic perspective I knew that, one way or the other, eventually everything would be okay.

"They'll miss you," Ra-u said.

"Yes, but they have a good father." I glanced at him as he continued.

"Yes, and he will keep them safe. But he will not teach them what you would teach them."

I looked back at their pictures again. "My children knew I was going to die when they picked me."

"Yes, but they also knew you would have a choice to come back and were hoping that you would."

As I watched more images of my children project into the sphere, the same surge of protective love flashed through my heart, yet never did I feel any pressure to pick one way over the other. Anyway, I still had more questions.

Ra-u and the others smiled at each other. They read me so well.

He continued. "Everything is in a state of grace; it will eventually all turn out well. Let's talk about any other questions."

"What will I do if I stay here?" I asked.

Meena smiled and turned to the sphere once more. "Let's show you what you did."

A large square room popped up in the wavy lines, a place with peach-colored walls and a timbered ceiling. Devoid of any furniture, one table stood in the center of the room. A group of light beings viewed a screen that lay flat on top of it. I could see myself from the back. I recognized my cap of curls and the dress I was wearing. A thought flashed through my brain: do we ever change clothes or is this for recognition?

The image zoomed in on the screen upon which a map of India stood. Tiny, bright yellow, blue, or lavender lights clustered around cities. Each light represented a light being that volunteered to incarnate and now lived on earth.

"For eons, higher souls, like Elders, incarnated near each other so they could intensify their light." As Meena spoke, the image faded and I looked at her. "Bodhisattva" popped into my head.

"Yes," she said, "Bodhisattvas incarnated with the specific mission to elevate consciousness. These first Elders were born into families and cultures that recognized the innate sacredness of these children and found appropriate teachers for them. These volunteers also remembered who they were and sought their connection with the Divine to fulfill their mission of bringing enlightenment to the earth.

"They wound up living in and around monasteries, temples, synagogues or wherever spiritual people congregated. In tribal families, they joined a medicine or shamanic path. In their studies, they lit the way for others. They did not take part in the day-to-day life. Indeed, isolation protected them from the dense energy of the villages. Older souls who came down to teach had to live outside the town and could do little else in order to maintain the integrity of their visionary goals. They attracted semi-awakened souls so around these Bodhisattvas, crowds, and gatherings would grow into communities. Looking from above, we could see many people following spiritual guidance. However, what of the younger souls that hadn't felt the call yet? Is it best to leave them alone and let them work out their lives?

"By the 1860's, enough global mindfulness had been brought to earth to effect a change in humanity's collective thought. At that point, another plan evolved to reach people who lived outside the spiritual communities. Instead of incarnating into older families, a different group of Bodhisattvas came forth with another alternative mission. To be able to spread out and disperse more light, the new helpers incarnated into the families of much younger souls and as far away as possible from any evolved souls. Their background, their history, and wisdom, was hidden from them. Unlike the former Elders, these light beings had their memories blocked.

"In this mission, they had to accomplish several things. Imbued with unconditional love, they would be vulnerable to the younger souls' families; to their philosophies, and abuses. Many were battered and ill-treated: forgiveness was the key, and the more they had to fight for what they believed, the more they forgave their abusers. They were to transmute negative energy by resisting being indoctrinated into a fear-based life. Many had to absorb it and live it, all the while knowing deep within that this pathway was inherently wrong.

"Sometimes they incarnated into malevolent families that annihilated any light they sensed. Others were born into loving, kinder families who still learned the curriculum of their first incarnations. They taught isolated, fear-based teachings, teachings that pitted differing philosophies against each other. The light beings lived in turbulence and had to forgive repeatedly. We never placed them near each other but kept dividing the spaces up between the light beings.

"The longing for the Divine was much stronger in them than anyone in their families. Through no fault of their own, they felt like outsiders, whether it was from their families, their community, or even their entire culture. They would spend the first half of their lives alone, feeling isolated and unable to find a clique that they could join.

"Also, for this healing to succeed, these light beings were born into families from unfamiliar soul groups. They had to be completely alone in the dark. Their unconscious mission was to discover their inner light all by themselves, without any direct training. All throughout their lives, many teachers would pass by, hidden from view but dropping hints. It could even be as simple as a hummingbird hovering nearby or a line in a book or a song. The inner Divinity, which lies dormant in every single person, created a deeper longing for expression. Through the often painful journeys of self-discovery, these people forged channels of forgiveness never seen before and eventually found that constant peacefulness that existed in their hearts."

After so many downloads, my sense of emotional unrest returned, so we took another break. I closed my eyes and enjoyed the immense peace and joy that surrounded me until my vibration reflected all the love around me.

When I was ready, I opened my eyes. "So this is what I did with these other light beings in my soul group? And we all came down to earth?"

"No, not all," Ra-u answered. "About a third stayed behind to channel support. Most of the group is still on earth. The goal was to lead people from the fight or flight response to a heart-centered one. You would land in the shade just like the others you had so carefully placed. In silence, meditation, or prayer, you would all return to divine consciousness found within until you fully grasped your lessons. Just like the light beings you had planted, you were all being asked to follow in their footsteps, blindfolded."

"What happened to these beings that incarnated into this place ... this shade?" I asked.

"The first groups of light beings that incarnated into the younger families didn't fare well. The lack of light was all-encompassing. Most of them blew out almost immediately; some flickered for a while then disappeared as the older soul struggled to find their light within and failed. Some were killed for their differences or banished and died young. Others may have led a conventional life, yet, deep within, each felt a yearning for a level of happiness not based on external things like the body or the material things surrounding them. They had absorbed what their family or their community had laid down as law. If the rules were based on fear and excluded others, the older souls would be restless, knowing somewhere deep within that there was more out there, unconscious principles about unconditional love and, eventually, they would seek it. Don't forget, every single human on earth has a soul, a connection to the Divine. Younger souls have little contact with this spark. As they grow in life and develop hope, they become more aware, more loving, and then they have the opportunity to experience inner peace.

"We waited to see and then re-seeded in the same spot. Even if they died right away, the residue left behind strengthened the following attempt. By the early 1930's there was enough residue left over from the previous beings for the new volunteers' efforts to effect a permanent change."

As Ra-u spoke, he gestured back to the sphere. The image of India grew as the view zoomed closer to the cities. I could see my freckled hand holding a brilliant blue piece of energy the size of a grain of rice. I kept it over the screen and sensed the best spot to place it and, eventually, I set it on an oscillating spot twinkling on the map. I chose the place farthest from any other old soul or any new volunteers. An angelic being advised us. We all stayed focused, yet the ambiance was joyful, happy, even playful and ever hopeful.

The scene switched back to the incarnating souls in the Great Hall. Hundreds of them waited in silence. Angels and light beings assigned to that room coordinated the process of incarnation. As I watched this little movie, it became apparent that to absorb and clear negative energy, these helpers were alone for a long time and thoroughly experienced the pain of human forgetfulness. All during their lives, many different opportunities for spiritually transformative experiences crossed their paths. Eventually, they recognized that these were life lessons and fully devoted their attention to healing."

Meena explained my second job Upstairs. I helped to stage the life reviews for returning younger souls. "We want their return to reflect where they lived on earth. When older souls ascend, they return to their core group and reside with them. Younger souls have to acclimate, and this takes time.

"You help a returning soul's transition by fabricating scenes that reflect their life on earth until they can assimilate the process. You have a knack for reading their happy memories and manifesting a safe place, like if they had a delightful time baking in their grandmother's kitchen. Then the room looks like that particular kitchen and cookie smells waft through the air. Their primary guide may look like their grandmother at first. After they finish their transition, they go back to their soul group's area which doesn't look anything like their grandmother's kitchen."

Meena said, "If you stay here, you will return to your core group and your previous activities. If you chose to go back to earth, and remember this experience, you would have a difficult life as you integrate all this information. However, once you finish processing these memories, this time you will connect to a higher level of hope. You will find a healing center with many other light beings, healers all working for the same goal: hope and empowerment."

I said nothing and studied the table. Grains of wood curled into beautiful patterns. I traced them with my finger.

Meena continued. "The hardest work on earth will be recovering the connection to your immortal soul. Then you must interweave this with your human consciousness. You will remember all your lessons along the way. When you were a child in Chicago, and we visited, you had no conscious memory of your history here. If you go back now, and you remember everything, the memories will eventually become an inspiration."

All now waited for me to speak. I still could not decide and asked another question, "What about my children? I still don't understand why they picked me when they were aware of my future choices. Why risk it?"

Another method of channeling information entered my mind. I did not hear words or see pictures. The group's connection helped me to access a broader awareness. The information about how a soul chooses its incarnation began to unfold.

Each person has their set of lessons, their curriculum, which is hard for another to understand. Since most light beings live and work within a group, they incarnate to experience multiple angles of a particular life lesson. One may play the abuser role to another's victim; then they switch to learn opposite sides of the same incident. We pick our earth families based on shared goals: it is not about vengeance or payback.

Multiple levels of light beings come down to play different roles in our life. All the different stages exist in close proximity. Upstairs, the same levels hang out together, like in those different villages I saw as I approached. Some beings skip lessons, others linger longer and wind up with a different group from when they first incarnated. In every being's birth family, it will be fashioned from many different villagers, usually but not always, from the same realm.

Some views about reincarnation teach that karma forces us into human life against our immortal soul's will, so incarnation reads like a punishment. However, at the deepest level our life spark, our eternal self, wants to be here—to be here, there, and everywhere. It incarnates willingly and checks out just as quickly. In fact, mercy brings us here to experience grace and altruism. Learning brings development. The number one goal of the Divine is growth and connection.

As we evolve, our power not only transforms us, it changes others. The dense energy of the earth plane and the levels within an incarnated human make it challenging to receive healing energy from Upstairs. An embodied light being can heal someone with denser power since they exist on similar wavelengths.

"There are many levels of consciousness," Ra-u added. "New souls emerge from the Divine core and, as consciousness develops, the Divine expands. The human attitude towards perfection is that it exists and should be the final goal, but that would mean that, once attained, there wouldn't be any more growth. If this happened, it would create a stagnant, unchanging world. That would be sad and impossible. Life on earth evolves: it cannot do otherwise."

In my mind and heart, the information continued to download. Younger souls continually emerge from the Divine and pick a particular set of courses similar to the way each grade in a school has a different lesson plan. Light beings look at an area of their life in which they desire growth and experience but it is not assigned: it presents itself as a suggestion. If one soul wants to break a lesson into three or four lifetimes, and another wants to do three grades in one incarnation, there is no judgment, no favoring one over the other. However, those who choose the fast track take on an inordinate amount of suffering and hard work. Younger souls rarely take that pathway.

There is no competition Upstairs, no shaming, and no twisting of arms. One has time and infinite patience to work out these lessons. It is all highly individualized. The youngest ones brainstorm and accept guidance from older light beings. The intermediate levels want input from others but have more choices. The evolved souls have more volunteer missions. Rarely does anyone incarnate, even young souls, with only one purpose in their curriculum. Volunteers land where they will learn and grow. Any growth from any being, young or old, advances the human "unconscious mind" and connects it to the immortal soul. This energy is the bond that unites all sentient life.

Then I asked Meena and the group about evil people, people that had cheated or killed fellow humans on an appalling scale. Where do they go? Certainly not up here to bathe in all this light and selfless love.

Meena and Ra-u glanced at each other. Ra-u looked back at me and the love in his eyes deepened. "This is a delicate question. Those who are cruel and kill or subjugate others are treated differently. Evil hurts on a larger scale than what happens to the individual victims. Souls that initiate large-scale violence or abuses of their rights are damaged by their actions too. They return in a fractured state. Compassion must guide our reactions to this."

Another image appeared in the sphere. The healing area for a shattered soul was a small, austere room with such grim barrenness that I gasped aloud. It almost hurt. No music, no song, just utter stillness with something that resembles a white cocoon with bright blue-white ends. It hovered horizontally and reminded me of incredibly dense cotton candy. It produced a light so bright that I shut my eyes and turned away. Everything faded, and the energy separated back into crackling wavy lines.

"When souls who have gone so far off course return," Ra-u said, "they become enveloped and covered with a thickened healing light. They must restore themselves and mend before they can face their life reviews."

Certain light beings took care of that task. I had sensed the grief within the bubbles because, at the core, no soul wants to hurt anyone or any creature.

Ra-u continued, "They will stay like this until they heal. Other souls continuously bathe them in the brightest light and selfless love until they recover. Damaged souls rest in proximity to the Divine, even though they cannot sense the blessed energy. This treatment brings them back into a state of natural alignment. Victims of suicides are also bathed in love and wind up in a similar area and must heal before they reconnect with their soul group."

"Victims?" That choice of word puzzled me. "How can you call them victims? I can feel the compassion, but they did it to themselves."

"Yes, victims; victims of the circumstances they endured without the capability to generate enough hope to make it through. Incarnating with the lesson of no confidence is an extreme one reserved for more developed souls. Many people contemplate suicide, but, eventually, they turn away and do not go through with it. Others follow through, but they aren't punished for their weakness. However, their advancement falters. Their energy depletes and they stall.

"Eventually, all these damaged souls leave the recovery room and go into another building in which they discuss their next step. Most often, the one who hurt others changes their schooling before they return to earth. They must experience the other people's point of view, sometimes many times, before they choose a lesson plan. Then, after several lifetimes and more experiences, they will try again, at the same level, undergoing the same temptations again. For the souls that have committed suicide, they will be schooled again in generating hope within, and go back to try to finish what they left before."

Ra-u stopped talking. The groups' energy hummed as it balanced all around me. Everything was peaceful, and, at that moment, I thought once more of my children. In my mind's eye, I saw them crying. A surge of love spread throughout me and I knew I had to return. Suddenly the advice changed direction. Now they focused on the problems I would encounter, starting with my crumpled body and the long and painful recovery.

Ra-u said, "We're all happy that you are choosing to go back, but we want to make sure you understand the whole situation. You will have to unlearn some lessons, and you won't have any teachers for a while, just helpers. Because of the density of human consciousness, even though you will know of its existence, you'll struggle at times to find your light within."

Nevertheless, I felt buoyant. "I want to remember everything here, and all of you. I'm sure that will inspire me to continue. Can I still receive guidance from you?"

"Not at first," Meena answered. "There will be times that you will agonize because even though you will remember us, we will seem too far away and that separation will hit you hard. Few in your world will understand or support your search. These memories may even isolate you from others. You will struggle until you integrate the awakened immortal soul with the human mind. Human consciousness moves very slowly. It'll take a tremendous effort to remember, so be patient and persistent."

As they talked, I remember thinking, what are a few years to the Infinite? I thought it would be easy peasy and pass like a flash. I repeated my resolve to return. Smiles traveled around the table. We waited again in pure silence as steadfastness flowed through the group.

Meena suggested I take my college training, return to a career in psychotherapy, and add the gift of an Intuitive. After my experience Upstairs, I could no longer deny my spiritual path or my inborn gifts. Previously when I tried to share my intuitive side and faced ridicule, I dropped the conversation, hid that part of me, and stayed on safe subjects.

She said, "You have a gift of learning life lessons in the most unusual ways." In the sphere, another scene began to unfold. Years ago, I had a dog named Orion. He was a giant dog, tall enough to look me straight in the eyes when I sat at the table. We hiked in the nearby mountains of Albuquerque. He ran through the underbrush before returning to trot next to me. Then he would rush off to explore yet another noise. However, one day during our hike, I heard a terrible sound: Orion painfully wailing.

Struggling through the underbrush, I found him caught in a leg trap. He alternated between chewing on his trapped leg and howling. Pictures of chewed up animals' legs left behind in traps jumped to mind as I tried to figure out the best way to save him. Noting a pin in the unbolting spring, I approached slowly, softly talking to calm him. He stopped the biting and shivered as he watched me approach. I assumed he had settled down and would let me help him.

As I reached for the button, he saw my hand close to his wound and lunged. A massive set of fangs came towards my face. I turned back but not far enough. His teeth sunk into my shoulder as he shook me like a rag doll. My jacket shredded which allowed me to escape. The trap's chain, attached to a log, stopped him from pursuing me. For a few seconds, he snapped and snarled at me. Finally, he turned back and began to chew on his pinned leg again.

Fortunately, another hiker heard the commotion and came crashing through the brush, calling out. He instantly sized up the situation, took off his jacket, and covered Orion's eyes. Then he pulled the pin, and the trap's jaws sprung open. Seconds later, Orion limped over, whimpering and seeking comfort as if his attack had never happened.

My reaction to Orion's attack had turned into a crucial life lesson. I was not angry with him for biting me. I understood why it had happened. I had been forced to jump into a dangerous situation.

The moment the trap closed on Orion's leg, he changed from my beloved pet into a wild animal struggling for survival. He was not my loving dog raised from a puppy whose adoring eyes always said "Mommy" when he looked at me. Orion reacted with his primitive, fear-based brain. It was the flight/fight reflex.

The encounter represented an excellent example of transference. When Orion attacked me, he unconsciously diverted his attention from the trap's teeth in his leg. With his teeth in my shoulder, the trap still gripped him. All the nerve endings connecting his foot to his brain screamed pain, yet Orion remained oblivious. Even when he chased me, the trap pulled at his leg, unheeded. Pouncing on me for those few seconds transferred his pain to another source, my shoulder, and he reacted as if the trap did not exist.

"Do you remember when this happened?" Meena smiled and asked. "That is what I mean about learning from the events in your life. You were never angry for the attack. You understood the core motivation: fear; fear and survival. After that, you applied that to other people in your life and quickly learned not to take things personally. Understanding what prompted their abuse helped you to tap into deep levels of empathy for others' pain that was their motivation for any personal attack in the first place.

"Think about what you can teach from this one experience. You will teach people how not to take things personally and, as you begin to clear yourself, you can turn your epiphanies into other life lessons. After all, you have seen and lived through; you won't deny what you know anymore. You won't want to. When you went to college, you studied with people from the medicine path along with psychology, the fine arts, and the sciences. Spirit and science have always been joined up in you. As you find a way out of the quagmire of illusion, of the separation from your spiritual self, write it down and teach it. Just as you had seen us as a child, help will turn up when appropriate. We cannot answer every question as it is your lesson to assimilate the separate parts."

I had to have a certain level of spiritual clarity before they could connect with me again. I had been a part of a healing process Upstairs. Now, the more I grew, the better I could help in both worlds. Meena said that, like many people on earth, I had a leg in both the spiritual world and the material world.

Once healed, I would always be connected to my inner light, my inner divinity. It is an aspect of consciousness that is latent within every single human being. If souls have too many answers, there would be no soul growth. After all, I came down to learn this lesson and no condensed versions allowed.

The room became soundless. I nodded and confirmed my commitment to return. Ra-u and I got up from the table and he led me towards the back wall. The undulation on the wall wasn't water after all; it was energy and was the entryway into what appeared to be a closet-sized room.

Next to it, sat a puffy pale apricot chair. Ra-u motioned for me to sit in it. Everyone smiled and said goodbye. I smiled back but felt choked up. Words would not come. As Meena touched her heart, a flash of love registered in my chest. Ra-u waved his hand, and my chair rolled through the lines.

The room had looked small, but the space was more extensive than it had seemed. Soon an undulating force buzzed all around me. Gradually I tingled all over. The energy particles felt like prickly bubbles. Everything in the other room became slightly blurred. The soft, beautiful music and singing which had faintly followed my every step now faded into one single note, a one-pointed note that gradually deepened and pressed against my ears. It increased and pulsed as all the space between the particles I had felt right after I died started to come together. From every fragment of my consciousness, density seeped in. I felt as if I was being squeezed into a sausage casing. I gasped. Ra-u reacted to my distress and stopped the entire process. The pressure subsided, and the sound stopped.

"Are you sure you want to return? You don't have to go back. You can stay; you have done enough. There's a lot to help with here too. Please don't go back if this is going to be too difficult."

I hesitated then shook my head. "No, I'm ready to go."

Ra-u smiled. Infinite love and support radiated from his eyes. He leaned forward and gently said, "Remember, every breath is precious."

"Maybe the distance between life and death isn't as great as you think. Maybe it's not that great chasm that you always thought it was ... maybe it's only a bridge."

~ *Morrie Schwartz*

Chapter Four

There and Back Again

itch-blackness surrounded me; severe pressure squeezed me from head to toe. I inhaled sharply, but my breath was stuck: I could not exhale. I could not move ... then, boom! A soft bump suggested that I had landed back in my body. The process of returning ended and I felt no pain.

I opened my eyes. A powder blue sky greeted me, a sky that seemed flat and featureless. Two men knelt next to me, and two women stood on my right. The feed barn's roof, the feed-box, and the fluttering leaves of two treetops were in my peripheral vision. When I finally exhaled, my conscious mind slipped away into shock.

My body lay still. No one had covered me with anything. All CPR had stopped. One of the men had told the cowboys to go and find Bob; I was "gone." Ranch guests and several cowboys gathered around me, silently waiting for Bob. What happened next surprised everyone. Unexpectedly, I moaned, sat up straight, and started to speak.

As Don O. later described it to me, "your skin was grey and your lips were as blue as your jeans." Then, as I gasped and sat up, one of my sunglasses' lenses popped out. No one noticed or removed them the entire time I talked. Our conversation went like this:

"Lesley! Lesley! Are you okay?" Everyone spoke at once.

"Of course I am," I said.

The man who had tried resuscitating me quieted everyone. He said, "Let's start at square one. Do you know your name?"

"Well, everyone's calling me Lesley, so that must be it," I answered as I leaned over slightly to my right.

Several questions later, they realized that I thought I was in Chicago and sixteen years old. When Bob arrived, I thought he was my father.

"Okay, just relax," the man continued, "I think we need to take you to the hospital."

I leaned further down onto one elbow and declared, "No, I'm fine! I'm fine. I don't need a doctor."

Bob knelt down and took my hand. Everyone tried to convince me that a hospital visit was vital.

"I want to go home. I'm not going to the doctor!" I remained adamant. By then I had slumped down onto my back. Still protesting, I passed out.

Soon EMTs had me strapped onto a portable stretcher. They secured my head to prevent any movement. Inside the ambulance, they attached an IV and, because blood had run out my left ear and nostril, they hyperventilated me as they drove carefully over the hilly road to town.

At the hospital, emergency room personnel checked me in and put together a battery of tests. The prognosis from my first two CAT scans was dire. The subdural hematoma went through the entire left side of my brain. Air bubbles were present inside the skull. The doctor assigned to the case told my family that there was a probability that I would die in the next day or two. If I did not die from the injury, I might never wake up but could continue indefinitely in the current comatose state. Even if I did come around, the hematoma's severity was likely to leave permanent damage. I would be lucky to have the mental facility of a four-year-old.

For ten days, I went in and out of Intensive Care, sometimes comatose, sometimes awake but still wholly amnesiac. On the days that I was out of the ICU unit, my friend, Sally D., told the staff that she was my sister and came into my hospital room with people that practiced alternative healing techniques.

Dr. Lila F., my "sister," gave me the homeopathic remedy Arnica Montana for shock and bruising. My "brother" Dr. Lance M. gave me cranial sacral treatments. During one session, something gently pulled me to the surface. I have one short memory of glimpsing Dr. M. as he sat above my head. He smiled down at me and patted my hair. It was dark in the room with one light behind him that made him look as if he had a halo. I smiled back at him and slipped back into the coma.

Eventually, I stayed out of the coma. The hematoma had damaged the regions in my brain most closely associated with my episodic and declarative memory, which included all my autobiographical information.

In addition to retrograde amnesia, I also had anterograde amnesia. I would remember the daily reality orientation, the date, the city, or reading clocks, for an hour or two. But by the end of the day, I could not recall what we had discussed. Every day we started over from scratch. I did not recognize photos of anyone in my family including myself. In addition, I did not remember looking at them.

The doctor suggested bringing my entire family into the room, including my children. He thought that might trigger my memory. Our nanny, Beatriz L. carried Cale who wiggled in her arms. He cried when she entered the room with everyone. Then again, he also cried when she tried to return to the lobby, so the two of them waited in the doorway.

I do have one fleeting memory of that day. Brenna pushed her way through all the adults and stood by my side. Grabbing my hand, she pleaded with me to come home; she was ready to take care of me. She said her kitty would keep me company and gave me her favorite stuffed white cat that I clutched. It became my security blanket.

Unfortunately, that was the same moment when the first of four Grand Mal seizures started. Bob dashed out to alert the nurses. Already traumatized to see me bruised and barely recognizable, my family watched helplessly as violent muscle spasms took over my body. Nurses raced in. One pushed them out of the room while the other two pinned my arms and lifted me onto a gurney.

Immediately I moved to the ICU again. Over the next three days, I underwent two more CAT scans to check how the seizures affected my brain injury. When the doctors reviewed them, they discovered that the subdural hematoma had spread even further. It had traveled both to the right hemisphere of my brain and down into my brain stem. I stubbornly clung to the stuffed cat, but no one bothered about it. No one in the medical team thought that I would recover.

Eventually, I surprised them all by waking up again, but I was not out of the woods. When questioned, I still believed I was in Chicago. At first, my level of articulation and conversation put my intellectual process slightly above a four-year-old. My doctor posited that with the severity of the brain injury, I might end up with the mental capacity of an eight-year-old. I was unlikely to regain my memory.

A couple of days after that, I picked up the telephone and found a sympathetic outside operator who helped me track down an old friend, Cher N. The only information I could tell her was that Cher lived in the same New England city as a famous Russian author. I said it was an emergency and that I had to speak with her. Since the operator could tell I was calling from a hospital, she took my request seriously and doggedly searched until she tracked Cher down in Cavendish, VT.

As soon as I heard her voice, I dissolved into tears. I told her that I had woken up all alone in a hospital. Since I could not construct a memory, I thought no one had told me why I was there. Nor would they let me leave. At that point, I said that I thought of her and called for advice.

Cher, a trained psychotherapist, calmed me down. She kept telling me that she was there with me, even though we only spoke through the phone. She said that she was not going to hang up until she heard me laugh.

She masterfully worked in a few questions about the date and current events. My lack of coherent responses let her know that I had suffered a brain trauma that included memory loss. She gently guided the conversation to my children. When I asked her what she meant by children, she dropped the subject.

She spent an hour telling me about living in Vermont and her day-to-day life. From time to time, she wove in stories about when she had lived in Lake Forest, a suburb of Chicago. We had been next-door neighbors for two years. When I finally laughed over the anecdotes, she said goodbye with a promise to call me every day.

As soon as we hung up, she called Bob. He explained what had happened and paraphrased the doctor's prognosis, stating I may only have the mind of an eight-year-old and never regain my memory. She disagreed. She said my conversation kept up with hers and pointed out that since I had not met her until I was nineteen years old, his diagnosis of my memory was probably wrong. I had remembered my past enough to find her.

Week by week, my brain improved. As the anterograde amnesia faded, a linear memory base formed. People, dates, news, and things like knowing the time of day connected me to the day before. The retrograde amnesia stayed, but while my history remained hidden, my recollections of Upstairs were as fresh as when they had happened. Every minute was still vivid, and whenever I recalled even a small part, it filled me with joy. Repeatedly, I would remember Ra-u and his last words: remember, every breath is precious. Now, gratitude implanted in me, it was so easy to be thankful for the caring team of nurses and my friend's and family's visits. Even after I had upsetting conversations with my doctor about my trip Upstairs, all I had to do was close my eyes, and it was as if I had returned up there inundated with the peacefulness, the joy, and selfless love. For that, I was eternally grateful.

My experience was impossible to describe, yet I longed to share it and to speak to someone who might be interested in what happened after I died. The light and love were still around me, but no one would listen. My husband, my mother, and my mother-in-law told me that it had been a beautiful dream but had no bearing on my life now. The doctor had told them all it was, at best, a hallucination, at worst a psychotic break. If they encouraged me, who knew where it would lead?

I was astonished. I had just experienced an extraordinary miracle and everyone tried to diminish it, to sweep it away, yet it had elevated me and filled me with immeasurable joy. It was real, ultra-real and had happened to me. I could not forget it. There was never a moment that I doubted the veracity of Upstairs. It was not just the visual memory—it was the sense, the knowledge that it had happened. The more I insisted, the more anxious they became. My family loved me, I knew that, but they were afraid for me. If I broached the subject, they would surreptitiously glance at each other. Quickly someone would pat my arm, murmur comforts, and change the subject. I winced at their pity.

In the end, my doctor intervened. Every icy gray hair lacquered into place, he walked into my room one evening and pulled up a chair, his face stern and his brown eyes unsmiling. He tersely launched into a lecture about psychotic hallucinations and followed-up with a grim warning: if I persisted with my delusion, he would have me declared mentally incompetent.

My stomach dropped. The doctor frightened me. Everything was such a muddle in my life. All I had was the few things I could remember. When I tried to speak, he turned his face away as he held his hand up to dismiss any further discussion. "I'm serious. If I hear that you have said even one more word, I will transfer you to a psychiatric hospital for the rest of your recovery. I will pump you up with so many drugs that you will not know if it is day or night."

Heavily medicated; he said it twice. Helpless and choking back tears, I finally shut my mouth. He could do it! He could do whatever he wanted to me. I could not remember anything about my life. That in itself was very unsettling. Unable to fend for myself, I shut down completely.

The nurse in the room fiddled with things in the cupboard until the doctor left. She came over and patted my arm. I burst into tears. She told me that occasionally, patients had told her of similar experiences. She brought another nurse the following night, and they sat on my bed and asked me some questions. It was nice to share, but they could only stay a few minutes. After that, whenever one of them was in my room, I felt a sense of hope when they would smile at me or pat my arm again.

Those last few weeks were the most difficult in some ways. Yes, I was stronger, but I was tired, too tired to read. I had a TV in my room, but there was little on that interested me, so I lay drifting in and out of naps. The stiff fabric of the hospital gown, smelling of bleach, kept me from resting comfortably. A physical therapist came into my room every day to teach me to walk again. The automatic balance inherent in our arms swinging in opposition to our legs was difficult at first, but, after several days, I could do it unassisted.

Messages over the intercom went on twenty-four seven, and the beeping of everyone's machines created a constant background noise. The ever-present antiseptic smell hovered throughout the ward and permeated the food. It never was dark: lights, wheels squeaking at all hours, and the constant murmur of others kept me awake. Tanque Verde's executive chef Harland B. packed meals for me daily, which was a relief.

My mother had come to Tucson two weeks before my release from the hospital to help me prepare for my return home. She was a trooper. She visited every day, loaded down with different bags, albums, and childhood memorabilia that went back three generations. She began with my grandparents and, as she showed them, she gave me the details of where they were born, where they were married, and how many children they had. That led to photos of my aunts, uncles, and cousins. I did not remember the people's names the following day, so she would start over until I memorized the details. My ability to learn and repeat the data was just that: me spewing facts. I could not look back and fondly remember any connection as I gazed at the photos, even though my mom gently reminded me with detailed anecdotes.

After I had learned about my extended family, she opened up her next treasure trove. We started with her wedding album. She showed me pictures of her wedding, my relatives, and my father so many years ago. Then she took out baby pictures of my siblings and me after which she placed them in the proper birth order. Next, I saw photos of our house and vacation pictures of our family sailing, fishing, or doing whatever we did as a group.

Finally, she brought out only pictures of me. Mom started with my baby pictures, then my First Communion, from high school all the way to college. In addition to the photos, she had kept many of my "firsts;" all my report cards and homework assignments from first grade. She recited details about my first job at the Pavilion nursing home, my first apartment in Evanston, and my first trips abroad—all in the hopes of producing an aha moment which would open that padlocked door to my history.

Daily she came in with lists and daily I struggled to remember. Emotionally, I drifted without an anchor. Memories that had woven my sense of self, my identity and my connection with humanity were gone. These images had woven a safety net with which I could navigate my life. Now the net had been ripped open, and I had slipped through, dropping through dark space with no place to land. Without them, instead of liberation, I was a nonentity, isolated from everyone.

My failure to remember terrified me. To lose all memory, to drift along without any identity made my stomach upset. Many times, I would break into a sweat and gasp to catch my breath when my mind remained blank. Told who I was, day in and day out, felt like waking up in a bad episode of the Twilight Zone. A person I did not quite know placed photos one by one on the roll-up table by my hospital bed. They could have been paintings in an art history test. Yes, I could recite the names, but that was all I could do.

Day by day, lovingly and patiently, Mom put out more pictures and prompted me with more anecdotes. Behind the love in her eyes, I could see fear, her sense of helplessness, as the lessons continued to fail. The doctor pressed my mom to push me for longer times even though she was concerned about how anxious I became.

Nothing connected me to any cache of memories. The only memories I had of my children were from Upstairs when Ra-u had shown me an image of them crying.

One day Mom had enough of my struggle and spoke back to the doctor. When he popped in, she stood up and told him she was giving me a break. She said she would only dip into the bag of photographs if I asked about them. She knew I had loved Agatha Christie, so, instead, she told him she was going to read a compilation of short Miss Marple stories to me. He said nothing, just turned and left. My mom continued to read to me when she visited, but when she was gone, time ticked by in slow motion.

My healing continued to surpass the doctor's predictions, and, in the first week of June, I finally went home. Concerned that the pressures and responsibilities of child rearing could cause a relapse, Bob had reserved a guest room for me near our house. The plan was for me to rest there for a month before I went home.

Balloons and flowers from all the family and guests filled the room. Trembling at the crowd that met me at the parking lot and walked me to the room, I was happy to jump into a regular bed with no antiseptic smells and no noises.

Mom brought Brenna and Cale over for daily visits, but my daughter, Brenna, needed more. She never forgot her pledge to take care of me and argued every day when Mom said it was time to go home. After the first week, Brenna refused to leave my bedside. She pushed my mom away, but I was tired and needed to nap.

Mom tried coaxing her away. When that did not work, she took Brenna's hand and tried pulling her towards the door. Brenna kicked her shins as she screamed to leave her there. Cale burst into tears. I realized that the separation was too much for my children, so I got up, walked the short distance to my house, and headed for my bed. Of course, I had to get past my dog Bosco, a 125 lb. Bouvier des Flanders. Happy to see me, he jumped and wiggled so much that he almost knocked me over. Soon, I climbed into my bed and snuggled with my children. I was home.

From then on, Bosco positioned himself in the doorway, which made it difficult for visitors to enter the room. During the rest of my recovery, he would lie there and softly growl at any adult who stepped over him, including my husband. Bosco let them know that he was there and watching. My children were fine. When Brenna or Cale crawled over him, they would get a snuggle and a lick.

From then on, Brenna delivered my meals. She carried them carefully, cautious not to spill a drop. Vaulting Bosco became a challenge, especially as his nose went on alert whenever food was involved. Most times, he nudged the plate; more often than not, something would slide off into his open mouth. By trial and lots of error, Mom learned to fill the glasses halfway up and quarter-portion the plates. That kept Brenna busy as she ran back and forth bringing me my meals and returning with empty plates and cups.

Reconnecting emotionally with my son, Cale, presented a formidable obstacle. On the day of the accident, I had held him while we ate lunch. We laughed and cuddled before I put him back into his highchair. I had told him that I was going down to the Tack room to help unsaddle. We played peek-a-boo, and then I said I would be right back. However, I never returned. The "right back" dragged on for almost three months, fully a quarter of his entire life. By the time I returned, he had treated me like a scary stranger.

Beatriz was a champion: she stepped in to help, day and night, with Brenna and Cale during my hospitalization. She loved them and treated them as if they were her own. They could not have made it through the trauma of a disappearing mom without her. The ranch had one hundred percent occupancy and then some. Bob had his hands full—taking care of everyone's needs, covering all my departments, answering questions, and keeping in contact with the hospital. Beatriz took care of the children every day of the week. Both Brenna and Cale came to rely on her.

When I returned, Cale still stayed in the doorway. He did not want to be close to me, yet he did not want to leave. Beatriz alone could bring him into my arms. If anything frightened him, he would run to her, or even Brenna, instead of me.

Patiently and persistently, I read with my children every day. Then, a couple of weeks after I returned, he jumped into my arms first as he climbed up on the couch. An important task now was to convince him that I would never vanish again. If he looked up and noticed that I had walked into another room without telling him, he would become hysterical, but at levels above a typical separation response. If I told him my destination, he would be okay, as long as he knew first.

Fortunately, a family friend, Naia A., a child psychologist who specialized in children with PTSD, instructed us to ignore any advice that suggested he should cry it out alone. She told me that if he became panic-stricken, hold him tight and rock him gently. Communicating with him was imperative, even if I sang lullabies or repeated silly rhymes. Keeping a soft, playful tone of voice settled him down. It took almost a full year for him to develop confidence in our relationship again.

With the severity of my injury and the ensuing retrograde amnesia, I needed a rehab program. Two weeks after my release, I returned to a rehab facility next to the hospital and, for over two hours, took a series of tests to determine how the injury affected my brain functions.

The following Monday, Bob and I went in to confer with my doctor and the therapist assigned to me. As we sat in a consultation room, my doctor walked in holding a thick red file. He reiterated that it was a miracle I was not dead or severely retarded. Never in his practice had he seen anything like it, yet his face was grim. However happy I might feel over this, he continued, my test results were dismal in several areas. The scores also indicated to him that I would probably have amnesia for the rest of my life. That was what he had expected given the severity of the quadruple fracture and the size of the subdural hematoma. He had a plastic coated diagram of a skull and drew on the picture to illustrate the range of the broken bones. It centered above my left ear and radiated in four directions from there.

The worst damage was to the frontal lobe, which plays an essential part in processing short-term memories and retaining longer-term memories, and to the temporal lobe that also figures in the formation of future long-term memories. Further damage was evident in the medial temporal lobe, the part of the brain involved with declarative or explicit memory—the memory you can instantly recall.

Because of the Grand Mals, there was a good possibility that I would never get my driver's license back. Since there was no way to predict if I would have another seizure, the doctor would keep me on anti-seizure medication. At the end of my therapy, he would revisit the issue to see if there were any changes to his long-term prognosis.

He pulled out my CAT scans and showed me how far the subdural hematoma had spread, the air bubbles in my brain, and how, after the Grand Mal seizures, the breakdown of tissue had spread over into the right hemisphere and down into the brain stem.

He then drew out several color-coded diagrams, several photos of other brain scans, and my CAT scans. He used these charts to explain how bruised brain tissue atrophies. The doctor did not think an MRI was necessary. Most likely, I would have several empty holes in my brain. In the other photos, the brains looked like Swiss cheese. On my CAT scan, he traced his pen over the section he felt would have these holes. It was two-thirds of my left hemisphere. A chill ran through me, and I shuddered.

In addition to the physical complications I had faced, there were psychological and emotional setbacks that often happened to brain-injured patients. Many who have injuries much milder than mine experience a multitude of personality problems. That meant I might suffer bouts of intense, irrational anger bordering on hysteria, confusion, and unpredictable behavior. In addition, many are influenced by impaired impulse control that could lead to verbal attacks and/or physical aggression. On the other hand, my executive function (which refers to the group of skills used to make decisions, problem solve and self-monitor) could be impaired.

Brain injuries can also contribute to psychiatric issues like depression, severe anxiety, and obsessive-compulsive disorders. They can even cause substance abuse. I asked how long would it take for these conditions to manifest. Since it was now three months after the injury, I persisted to get my question answered. If I had this kind of damage, would I see the symptoms? Alternatively, is it something that would occur later?

He did not answer. He shuffled the papers back into the file and finally said he did not know; usually that kind of behavior showed up immediately. He then outlined his recommendation for the therapy needed to regain whatever brain functions remained. He said that the injured part could not recover. He promptly excused himself when he finished.

After the doctor left, George S., the therapist assigned to my case, entered. He introduced himself and shook both our hands. He flipped open a manila folder and took out my test results. He mentioned that he had met with the doctor earlier that morning. With the severity of the injury and the low scores, he felt it would be best for me to come three times a week with two-hour appointments each time. He added that it would probably be at least ten months to a year before I would finish all the study levels.

The following Wednesday Bob dropped me off for my first session. George mapped out what he felt were realistic goals for the upcoming months. He glanced at the test of identifying pictured objects, the one in which I had scored a measly twenty-four percent. I could define the objects' essentials with precision, but I could not think of the name.

I laughed as I remembered the pictures. "I cannot believe that I could look at a camel and forget its name. I love animals. I know what a camel is."

"You remember that?" Puzzled, George looked back over the list and asked, "Do you remember what else you missed?"

"A pair of tongs, a trowel, a lamp, a rose, a shovel, a trellis, an abacus ..." I rattled off the objects that I had failed to identify.

"I'm surprised that you can name all the photos you missed," George said. "It typically takes patients much longer to retrieve such information, even the immediate memories. In your case, I didn't expect you to remember anything this quickly."

"Oh, good! Can I go home?"

"No, let's move on to the exercises." George laughed. We passed the afternoon using different computer programs centered on repetitive patterns. Other programs required solving logical problems by remembering facts and sorting out numerical sequences.

Every time someone picked me up, George reevaluated the length of time required to pass all the tests. Referring to his initial assessment, he said that I might not need a year. After two more sessions, his prediction was eight months; that then became four months, which, after another meeting, became two.

Three and a half weeks later, I finished all of the tests and programs that he had set out for me. George said that he had never had anyone do it in fewer than six months so he asked if I would add two more weeks to try some higher-level challenges. I passed them, too.

On the last day, as we reviewed the past few weeks, George explained that the rest of my lost memories were not necessarily gone forever. Because of my quick recovery, he had a different opinion of my prognosis. Perusing old pictures, listening to the music I loved as a child, especially as a teenager, or sharing a personal history with friends and family, would help me to find all those "locked closets" as he called them. George stressed the word patience; it would take time: maybe even a couple of years. I had not lost the keys; I had just misplaced them.

When the locked door swung open, almost all of the memories would return, but it would not be just as simple as if one or two pictures would pop into my mind. The flashbacks would flood in like a slapdash slide show. All the first emotions tied to the incident would also return. The happy memories would make me over-giggly, but George warned me to prepare myself because it could be overwhelming when the memories were from painful experiences. As alarming as it might feel at the moment, I would also process them within a few hours to a few days. "Try to think of it like pulling off an old bandage. It hurts briefly for a few minutes; then you bounce back to normal."

George patted me on the back as he walked me to the door. I hesitated. The doctor's words about personality disorders still haunted me. In spite of the fact that he had said those signs usually present themselves immediately, he had not sounded inspiring. Even though I feared the answer, I decided to ask George about how brain damage can affect one's behavior or psychological well-being.

George moved back to the table and pulled out a chair. He sat down with me as he spoke. "With all of the testings that you have gone through and the rehabilitation, if you had that kind of damage, we would have found it by now. It is more than three months after the head injury, and you have taken up your life again. Other than the retrograde amnesia, you are having no trouble adapting to feeling love, being happy and remembering things. Look how quickly you went through these tests! No one in my experience did that before. Please, Lesley, don't worry, there's nothing wrong with you."

The doctor still would not agree to validate my license. He stalled because I finished my rehab too quickly. He said he needed more time to make sure my brain had healed and instructed me to continue taking the anti-seizure medication for two more years. I had taken it for five months and experienced unhealthy side effects, one of which brought me back to the ER. A vein in my right arm ballooned up, and the last two fingers on my hand became paralyzed. I worried about a vein ballooning up like that in my eyes or brain. He had put his hand up to stop my questions so many times that I decided that I needed a second opinion.

I went back to Dr. Lance M. He researched the doctors, and after another two weeks, he suggested another neurologist who practiced at the University of Arizona Medical Center. When I made my appointment, I said that I needed a second opinion regarding my recovery from a head injury. The nurse asked if I would allow neurology students to observe. I agreed at once. In that type of environment, perhaps I could get in a question or two of my own.

The hospital sent my records over, and I brought my CAT scans with me. I had not received any notification that revoked my license, so I had driven myself. As Doctor S. slid them one by one onto the lighted viewing board, several students crowded around. I sat on the examination table and watched as the doctor chatted with them. When all the images were up, he stopped and quietly stared at them. He looked at the dates, reorganized them, and took a few more minutes before he turned and asked, "This is you?"

"Yes, why would I bring in someone else's?" I laughed.

"And you drove yourself?"

"Yes … I did." That question worried me.

He turned back to the students and addressed the severity of the injury. If he had an unconscious patient with these CAT scans, he would expect the patient to remain comatose for an indefinite amount of time and, if awakened, to be severely damaged. He answered countless questions as to why. Every so often, he would glance back at me. After he had finished his analysis, he gave me a cursory examination that included some physical reflex tests, looking into my ears and eyes, and turned back to the CAT scans. It fascinated me to see a doctor that enjoyed teaching and sharing the information, and I watched as he pointed to various parts of the CAT scans. During the Q & A with the students, much of the discussion regarded what side effects were standard with that kind of hematoma. The discussion centered on how they might affect the behavior or primary cognitive skills.

He turned to me and asked if I had any questions. That was a nice surprise! At first, I could not think of anything. Then, I mentioned the other doctor's warning about the possible personality changes as a setback.

He replied to my answers with the same patience he responded to the students, though his explanations were less technical. He assured me that those problems were apparent almost immediately. Since I had not exhibited any of those complications during the past five months, it was improbable for them to start now.

He asked if I had brought my MRI. I replied no.

"Really? That's odd." He looked puzzled.

When a student inquired why, he pointed back to the CAT scan and, with many fancy words, described how brain tissue generally contracts to a degree as it heals, which leaves behind empty cavities. Then he pointed to me. "This level of recuperation does not correspond with this degree of injury. I've never seen a patient recover like this. I think an MRI is necessary for us to understand why." Therefore, he ordered one up.

He also answered my concern about another Grand Mal seizure. The doctor said he could not answer my concerns until my MRI showed how much brain tissue I had lost. Once I had it done, I would meet with a panel of doctors to discuss the prognosis. If I still needed medication, there were other options.

A week later after the MRI, I brought my CAT scans and met with the Neurology group. My doctor showed everyone the MRI too. He pointed out that my brain tissue had not atrophied, which did not fit their expectations. They had discussed it at length that morning. Because my healing was outside the norm, they hesitated to let me keep my license without medication.

I asked them a simple question: if they had only seen the MRI, would they think that my brain was severely scarred and likely to have more seizures.

They agreed that the MRI was surprising. Based on the MRI alone, they did not expect residual damage.

"It's not my fault that I healed in a way you don't understand. Is it possible that my brain healed completely?" I waited for them to answer. They all agreed that it would be improbable for me to have another seizure. They finally decided that this was a unique case and subsequently signed off on my keeping my license.

I then asked about personality changes that many brain-damaged people experience. They said that was not the case with me. Behavioral problems usually occur right after the injury. I finally felt that I had a clean bill of health.

Gradually my strength had returned, and, instead of bone-tired fatigue and eighteen hours a day in bed, I began to get restless. We decided it was time for me to walk on the trails around the house.

One of the favorite events at the Tanque Verde Ranch is an early morning breakfast ride. Guests travel out on horseback through the Sonoran desert and wind up at an old homestead. There they eat an enormous western style breakfast cooked over a mesquite-fired grill. My home was a short walking distance from the cookout, so I planned to hike up the hill, meet the riders, and enjoy the feast. It had poured all night long, but, by morning, the rain had stopped.

I kissed my children goodbye and found the trail to the homestead. Radiant shafts of dazzling white light speared through the dappled gray clouds as they broke apart. Riveted, I understood why crepuscular rays had the nickname "God's rays." All over the foothills, shadows stretched out in front of each tree, shrub, and cactus.

I gazed up at the sky for a minute or two while the sun pleasantly heated up my shoulders, then I set off for the homestead. Halfway there, I turned. Somewhere off to my right came a distinctive sound. Last night's rains had caused all the gullies and ravines to fill up. Streaming water splashing through stony washes is a rare treat in the desert. I decided to take a brief detour to find it.

Raindrops covered everything around me. In awe of my surroundings, I stopped to examine everything I saw. Crowns of pink and white flowers peeked through the hooked spines on the Barrel cactus. Hedgehog cactuses' crimson flowers provided a startling contrast to the subtle sage-green desert grasses. Tall spikes of pink penstemon wildflowers waved in the breeze. Huge, stately saguaros topped with white trumpet-shaped flowers marched down the hills. Several had red-fleshed fruit picked open by the Gila Woodpeckers that flew by. Purple, red, or green flowers cascaded down cholla's spiny branches. Prickly pear cactuses had flowered earlier and now red fruit clustered on top of the pancake-shaped pads.

Little creeks ran all around the hills into the main wash while the water splashed and rippled. Countless water droplets glistened on the barbed wire fence that separated the different fields I traversed. Mini-suns shimmered inside each drop like diamonds. The rising sun lit the greenery from behind, which reminded me of Upstairs.

Entranced, I forgot my plans and meandered to the creek that flowed bank to bank. I took off my shoes and waded across to the other side.

After I had put my shoes back on, I came upon a mule deer mother and fawn. Love for life surged through me as I watched this mother and child. She grazed with her back to me. I walked closer to her and stopped a few yards away. She turned to look at me but did not flinch. The fawn darted around in front of the mother and peeked back at me, but would not come any closer. We stood in silence: I lost track of time. Then she looked over my shoulder for a brief second before she turned and quietly walked off. Her baby bounced along right next to her.

A minute later, I heard someone calling my name. When everyone else had arrived at the homestead but me, the wranglers jumped back on their horses and rode out in different directions to find me. The cowboy teased me about wandering off. He dismounted and gave me a leg up on his horse. He radioed the rest of the wranglers then took the reins to lead me back.

By the end of August, I returned to work. The process of familiarizing myself with the different departments that I oversaw would be long and tedious. I hauled out various thick folders that packed my file cabinet drawers. They all had different titles: Landscaping, Ranch Store, Wrangling Dept., Housekeeping, Children's Dept., Remodel, Design, ETOC, etc.

My mind was blank as I flipped through the paperwork, hoping that something, some picture or some scribbled sheet, would trigger the memory. Little by little, over many weeks, it worked. My struggles to return to a hectic multi-level job smoothed out as I slipped more and more into a repetitive work routine.

I had put my memories of Upstairs on the back burner and dedicated myself to relearning my life on the ranch. Even so, most nights I would think about my experience before dropping off to sleep. The reminiscences soothed me, and I promised myself that when my life had settled a little more, I would write it all down. I would remember. The closest explanation to my experience that I found was in Elisabeth Kubler-Ross's *Death and Dying*, which hinted at the possibility of receiving messages from people as they died. However, her book did not explain what I had encountered.

Returning to my horses was a different kettle of fish. One day I received a phone call from a man named Paul. T. Many guests still called to wish me well and, assuming that he was one of them, the switchboard put him through to my office.

A husky western drawl boomed over the line. "Lena's Lady is pregnant! I'll wait another week or so and then do the final blood test. I'll send her back to the same shipper we used before."

I looked at the handset, then put it back to my ear and said, "Pardon me? What are you talking about?"

He started to repeat the message then paused. "Is this Lesley Cote?"

I answered in the affirmative.

"Well, Lena's Lady is pregnant. Remember?"

"Who's Lena's Lady?"

"Your mare?"

"I have a mare?"

"Yes, you sent her here in March to breed with my stallion. Are you sure this is Lesley Cote?"

As soon as I heard March, I understood. As I explained what had happened, he howled with laughter and said it was the first time anyone had sent him a mare and forgotten about it. Apparently, I had shipped her off to be bred the week before my accident. Now, six months later, she was almost ready to come home. He hung up still chuckling, swearing he had a story to tell for the next twenty years.

Eventually, I had to get back on a horse and ride again. If an inexperienced rider approaches a horse and is afraid, the horse's radar-like instincts will notice that fear and it will become skittish. Therefore, I had to be calm and confident before I could ride again, both for my safety and for any friends or guests whom I might lead on a trail ride.

I had a two-year-old Andalusian gelding named Ari and, before my injury, one of the cowboys, Joe V., had trained me to halter-break him. Too young to ride, Ari had learned how to wear a halter and follow my lead. He and I had spent many an hour in the round pen and I had taught him how to obey commands.

I walked down to the corrals after breakfast. Brought up from the back pasture, Ari ran loose in the rodeo corral. Wranglers climbed up on the mesquite branch fence to watch over the situation. As I walked into the corral, Ari saw me and raced over. The sight of him thundering up frightened me. I crossed my arms over my chest, sucked in my breath, and braced myself as I closed my eyes. Two cowboys jumped down and ran towards us.

Ari got to me first. He halted a foot away, snorted and stomped his front leg. I peeked to see what was happening. He stood there looking at me. Then he calmly bowed his head and touched my forehead with his. He then nibbled my collar before bolting off, kicking up his heels and running around. For the next few days, I brushed his coat, mane, and tail and practiced cleaning his hooves. Under supervision, I brought him down to the round pen to school him on how to wear a saddle and bridle with a bit.

It was in the same rodeo corral a few days later that I got back in the saddle again. I had to pass the same test that every novice rider must take. To start, they selected a gentle horse: that is cowboy code for *very old* or *extremely old*. Chico was perfect for beginners because he only had two gears: *very slow* and *extremely slow*. They were not taking any chances.

A forty-gallon barrel stood twenty yards away from the gate. My test was to race up to it, maneuver the horse around it, and return to the gate as quickly as I could. My challenge with Chico was getting him to move more quickly than a slow shuffle. He did not mind traipsing down the trail, following the lead horse, but, to run around the barrels, even just one, was going to be a stretch.

It took quite an effort to get Chico to trot and to turn. I never even tried to make him go faster. Stopping was a breeze and quite funny. We laughed all the way through my first riding test. Chico did finally pick up the pace but not until he was turned out to the hay barn.

The next day I rode Comanche, a younger horse with a lot more spirit. There were three barrels, so I executed the standard barrel race pattern. I trotted, turned, loped, and stopped him until the wranglers were satisfied. Next, I rode in line with the guests, riding right behind the lead cowboy. After a week of this, we decided it was okay for me to ride by myself. Now I could go out on the trails with my friends.

Just as George had predicted, memories surged back, and the subsequent emotional highs and lows often felt like being superglued into a roller coaster. At the Tanque Verde Guest Ranch, the weekly guest return rate averaged sixty-five percent, which is exceptionally high. People always returned at the same time of the year, so, over the decades, families would meet other families and build long-term friendships. Every single week would be a mini-reunion for guests and employees alike. Our drivers had prepared the incoming guests by giving them an update on my recovery. I probably would not remember who they were, but that, with a little prompting, I usually did. Surrounded by an outpouring of love and support from these guests, who had known me for years, I felt protected. Many had been to my wedding, hugged me through my pregnancies, played with my babies, and shared meals with us at the Captain's table.

Every day, returning guests introduced themselves. They reminded me of their names and regaled me with anecdotes of our past. One by one, most of the memories of our histories returned. Sometimes I could not remember, but no one seemed to mind.

For several months, I would awkwardly freeze whenever I realized that I was meeting yet another person, another locked door. I would take a deep breath and paste on a smile as I shook their hands, hoping for that little flash of memory that unlocked the door.

Nothing terrified me more than the helplessness of having a void for a mind. Memories, good and bad, bolster our framework and give us the foundation of our identity. At that point, most of everything I knew about myself was merely a collection of facts, which I had learned from my family; they never originated from my knowledge, from my skills or capabilities, or from my proficiencies. By this time, the employees knew the bullet points of my personal history so they could field questions from returning guests concerned about my recovery.

A bizarre yet funny memory recall happened in the gift shop. Whenever they were busy, I popped in to give a hand. As soon as a guest ride returned, people crowded in to buy t-shirts, hats, or other Tanque Verde Ranch memorabilia, so every pair of hands in the office helped.

Before my head injury, I spoke French well enough to converse with the many Europeans who visited the ranch each summer. Bob had a gift for languages and spoke five fluently. During my recovery, he tried to revive my bilingual capability by repeating words and phrases in French. No matter how hard we struggled, that door stayed stuck.

One day we hosted a tourist group from France. The head organizer, Annette L., had brought many travel groups to the ranch over the years. When Annette arrived, she heard of my head injury. Yet she was unaware of the full extent of my memory blocks.

She came into the store as I was refolding T-shirts. She hugged me, kissed both cheeks and launched into a lengthy salutation. Since she barely spoke any English, in all the years before we had chatted in French. However, this time, even though I had no idea what she said, I answered her. Stranger still, I had no idea what I had just said and replied in complete sentences, not halting words. This time, no memories poured in with all my files on the French language.

We chatted like this for several minutes. Unknown French statements continued to come out of my mouth until Annette wished me well, kissed both cheeks again, and left the store. I was stunned. I could not even remember the words I had just used. My mind was blank.

Unsettled, I plopped down at the desk to figure out what had occurred. It ranked as one of the strangest experiences I had encountered. Perhaps because Annette expected me to respond, I did, even though I still had no idea what I was saying.

Annette saw Bob in the front office. She waved, and he walked over to say hello. She said, "I heard Lesley had the accident, but she didn't forget her French, no?"

Later, Bob came into the shop. I laughed and cried as I told him what had just happened. He tried once again to converse with me in French, but I still could not answer.

One August morning, Bob and I got a call to visit our next-door neighbors. On a ranch, next door means a half-mile walk to their house. The couple had initially stayed at Tanque Verde Guest Ranch before they bought the adjacent property for spring and fall getaways with their children. We walked through the cottonwood grove and crossed the dry waterway. Scrub brush and blooming cactus covered the desert. We approached their house situated in a grove of shrubs and trees.

Linda opened the door and greeted me with a hug and kiss on my cheek. I smiled back, but, as I walked in, I ran into another locked door. She did not look familiar; nor could I remember any of our previous visits. We went into their sunlit living room, our footsteps echoing on the blond wooden floors. Her husband was outside with their horses. I looked around the room dominated by a Baby Grand piano. Big windows opened out onto the Rincon mountain vista. With another sigh, I shook my head. It all looked so foreign. We sat down to tea, and, for the next few minutes, I answered questions about the accident and recovery. I explained that when the memories first returned, I would be at the same age when I first experienced them. Since we had known each other for five years, I thought it would be a breeze. Linda tried to help by describing our previous visits such as their horseback rides over to visit us.

Paul finally came in and walked over to hug me. I nodded to the piano and asked if anyone in the house played. Linda glanced at Paul and laughed. She said they both played and had even recorded a bit of music too.

"Would you like to hear it? Maybe that would help jog your memory." Paul went over to his bookshelf and flipped through some CDs. He asked me if I remembered any music from the sixties and named a few different bands, but none of them rang a bell. He turned back and said that he had played in a group.

"When?" I asked.

"Our first album came to the States in the early sixties. Beginning of '64, I think?"

"'64? That's so long ago. I was eleven." I smiled. "Would I still recognize it?"

He laughed out loud. "Now I feel old! But yes, I think you might remember."

Paul selected two CDs and handed them to me. I looked at them both, turned them over and shook my head.

He pointed to the one I had in my left hand. "This one's our first one. Anything?"

I looked at the black and white picture of four headshots on the cover. Still nothing. Paul walked over to the piano and patted the place next to him. I sat down facing Bob and Linda. He started with the beginning chords of the first song to see if it might trigger my memory. Not at first, but suddenly I remembered all the lyrics and sang the next few lines with him. Not only did I remember the song, I recalled which one came next and called out the title. Paul launched into it and we sang the first few lines. By the time we started the third song, snippets of screams floated up from my memories, continuous screams that surrounded me as I watched a film in a movie theatre. The sound was deafening, yet it was coming out of me too. As the picture in my mind's eye came into focus, it was four men playing in a band.

At that point, the door unlocked and started to swing open. It was not much; just a snippet of an unconnected memory, images from a long gone film. It did not need to be anything more than that to make me happy because, at that point in my life, any recall lit me up. I was encouraged. I could tell that I knew all his songs by heart.

We sang another couple of lines, and then the picture came into sharp focus. I stopped singing. I looked back over my shoulder towards the man playing, shocked at the memories that began to tumble out of the locked closet. Paul stopped playing. He tried not to laugh. Bob commented on the fact that he thought my memory had returned. The rest of my recollections began to arrive.

Broken-up bits of data scudded through my mind. I was sitting next to Paul McCartney. And he was singing—with me. Paul McCartney.

Instead of me being a thirty-one year old on the day we first met, my inner eleven-year-old hijacked the roller coaster of emotions. I inhaled sharply and blushed, my face and neck turned beet red. Linda and Bob laughed. I gasped. I stood up and sat back down. I stammered.

Paul hugged me again and remarked on how refreshing it was to be unknown. Linda asked more questions as I recounted some of the giddy girl memories that poured in from my infatuation with the Beatles. The first album I ever owned had been this very one: *Meet the Beatles.* My dad surprised me with it as a gift for getting on the honor roll.

We also talked about their appearance on the Ed Sullivan show and the never-ending earsplitting shrieks that came from the audience. The movie theater was a replay of their concert at Shea Stadium. We could not hear a single song because everyone just screamed until we were hoarse. The ticket stub, which I kept in my hand the entire concert, was crushed beyond recognition yet I held it for years, pressed in a book with flowers from my yard.

Linda recounted our visits to their farm south of London and suggested a few clues about the architecture and gardens. Eventually, that door opened too. I remembered their fantastic kitchen with the semi-circle of windows that overlooked their fields.

By the end of the visit, we were back on the footing we had before the accident. I did not stammer or blush when I said goodbye. Paul gave me the CD as I left and Linda gave me one of her cookbooks. One of the things I had recalled by then was that I, too, had been a vegetarian for the last few years.

Some of the experiences were not so welcoming. One day in October, a guest, Tim S., approached me as I walked up from the wrangling department. I was alone, but I stopped as I would for any guest. He said, "I heard about your accident and your memory loss. That must be so scary, but I think I can help you. I've been coming here for years, and you know me. We both lived in Oak Park, and I remember a lot of details about you when you were in high school."

I stood there, smile strategically placed, and allowed him to recount his history with me as I had done dozens of times with other guests. This time, however, no memory file came trundling out of the hidden closet. The door stayed locked. I did not recognize him, so he kept on adding more details. It would not have made a bit of difference. He could have told me that in Oak Park, all the houses were painted fire engine red and I could not access any truth, any fact, to dispute him. Through clenched teeth, I prayed for a miracle. The longer he spoke, the more the floor dropped out from under my feet, and I began a free-fall into a bottomless pit.

He asked where I had lived and I answered again by rote. He said he lived on the next street over and didn't I remember him? He said he could not remember if I lived east or west of his home, but now he did. He was two years younger, but we played together with his sister who was my age. He claimed to have had his first kiss with me when he was in the forth grade. Then he recounted how many times we had ridden together at the ranch.

I tried to hide my growing dread and thanked him for trying to help. The more he pressed me, the more I panicked. I felt a shaft of pain in my gut at the same time I felt a crushing weight on my chest: I could not breathe. The anxiety attack took over my body, and I trembled. My eyes teared up. He laughed and patted me on the shoulder.

"Oh, don't worry, you'll remember," he said as he walked away.

For the next few days if he found me alone somewhere on the property, he would add random facts about our desert flower ride, or the time we saw a rattlesnake and my horse spooked. Or he elaborated about our years at Oak Park High and hinted that we had more than just a friendship. After each revelation, he commented about how much fun it would be for me once I remembered. The more he persisted, the more terrified I grew. I tried to avoid him by eating in the employees' dining room.

The last time he cornered me, lunch had finished, and I headed over to the corrals. I wanted to check on the childrens' program. Tim was sitting in the TV room. He jumped up when he saw me enter. I tried to backtrack to an "Employees Only" door, but he caught my wrist and led me outside to ask me more questions.

One of the regular guests who supported me was also Bob's cousin, Susan H. She had walked out of the restaurant to have a cigarette. She saw us standing nearby, him holding my wrist and me standing with my head down, already in tears.

She ran over and pulled me away from him, hugging me tightly as she tore into him. "What the fuck are you doing?"

"What? I'm just trying to help her remember like everybody else," he said, struggling to defend himself.

"How could you?" She shouted, "You've never been here before!" Susan usually came three times a year and knew everybody including the new guests.

"Are you sure?" I asked. Startled, I looked at her. "He's been talking about the rides and such."

"It's only information that he knows from being here now. He's with that Chicago group, and this is their first time here."

Susan's anger caused him to flounder. He finally admitted that he did not know me. He stammered as he said, "No ... we ...we've never met."

Bewildered I was speechless. Never met me? That admission hurt me more than his harassment. How could anyone take pleasure in abusing a wounded person?

"What about Oak Park?" I asked.

"I didn't know you," he answered. "I went to Fenwick."

Swearing up a storm, Susan rebuked him for his actions. He begrudgingly apologized.

"Sorry," he mumbled to me, then turned to Susan. "What's the big deal anyway? Can't anyone take a joke? I didn't realize she might get upset."

"Her tears didn't give you a clue?" Susan said, shocked by his dismissive apology.

Over the next year, my memory roller coaster took me on numerous fluctuations up and down. For the most part, the locked doors opened gently. I developed a sense of history again. However, the roller coaster could also plummet down.

At a dude ranch, the prevailing theme is *Cowboy*. To that end, the local country-western radio station aired throughout the front offices twenty-four seven. One day the disc jockey introduced a singular song. He said it was an odd request for their station but that he would play it anyway. A few seconds later, Roberta Flack's voice began to float through the office as she sang "The First Time Ever I Saw Your Face."

The entire staff looked at each other. The song choice was curious. It was nice, but out of place, so they all laughed. Everyone but me. I burst into tears. Stunned, I ran back into my office. At the time, I had no idea why this song affected me in such a way. No door unlocked to give me a clue either.

Several days later, with no reference to the previous week, another disc jockey said he would play a special request, a little bit different from what they usually play, but what the heck. It was, in his opinion, one of the greatest love songs ever recorded. Therefore, he played the exact same song again—on a country and western radio station.

Again, a deluge of tears came, but this time as I ran back to my office, the locked door opened and I remembered why the song touched me. It was the love song a young man had chosen for us, a man I had loved but lost in a car accident when I was twenty-one.

In September of 1972 a mathematics student, Sean Z. transferred to the university I attended. Synchronicity caused our paths to cross. The first "get to know you" party was in full swing in the Rathskeller. The school had even sprung for a band. I stood on one side of the room talking to some friends. One of the overhead lights, reduced to a pinpoint, shone on the back of my head, backlighting my long wavy hair.

Sean pointed me out to his friend, John B. "Do you know her? The one with a halo?"

John confirmed he did. We had several classes together, and we played Spades at least twice a week. When he mentioned my name, Sean remarked, "I'm going to marry her."

Later, as John recounted the story, he told me how he had laughed, but Sean was resolute, so they came over for the introduction.

At first, Sean made no mention of romance, and we became close friends. We would meet for tea or walk around the campus, intimately discussing our world and its existence: Watergate, the terrorists at the Olympics, Wounded Knee, and the peace talks in Vietnam intermingled with reflections on our future goals. Life stood before us like an incredible mountain, begging to be conquered.

Within two months, his intentions deepened, and he proposed. He had invited me over to his home, saying he found a song that he wanted me to hear. Roberta Flack's melodious voice sang "The First Time Ever I Saw Your Face." The lyrics bespoke of heartfelt love, a spiritual, heavenly love in which all boundaries disintegrated between the lover and the beloved.

On one knee, he described the lightning bolt that struck the first time he saw me with my hair all-aglow. He knew then that he wanted to marry me but waited to tell me so as not to scare me off. His ideal life would be to have me as his wife, two Labrador Retrievers, and four children.

Even so, I refused. It was the early seventies, and the thought of turning into Laura Petrie was not a personal goal of mine. I wanted to define who I could be, to explore what I could contribute, and what career I might choose, in addition to, or instead of, marriage and children. I had signed up for a double major: a B.A. in Psychology and a B.F.A. in Studio Art.

I was also training off campus with two different metaphysical teachers: a Medicine woman named Lily R. and a Wiccan High Priestess named Bonnie D. I met these women within two weeks of each other. Both had said the same thing to me when we first met: "Why do you have your light turned off?" Somehow, even though I had shut down my childhood gifts, the intuitive light, which still lingered in my field, was recognizable.

They both offered to teach me how to deepen my perception without charging me a penny; it was a real apprenticeship. Since I had enough cash from my summer job to coast through the school year, I could take the time to pursue these less traditional educational opportunities.

I voiced my concern that his attachment happened too quickly, but I was not ready to walk away either. Sean laughed and said his proposal was not an ultimatum. He stated my father was not around to give him the opportunity of declaring his intentions. He was patient and could bide his time as long as I knew that our marriage was his goal.

I had developed a bond with him that I had never experienced before. Our relationship happened in the early seventies. In the midst of the "war of the sexes," he treated me like an equal, a best friend, and with respect. He had no game and never bossed or bullied me. It would have been impossible to boss him back. That was exceedingly difficult to find at that time. Quietly, I appreciated his declaration but chose to wait and see if he was for real.

More memories surged in: all the quirky things he did for me—filling my dorm room with thirty helium balloons in various colors or with two dozen floral bouquets and a handmade big red cut-paper heart on Valentine's Day. One day as I came back to my dorm room after class, I noticed that the housemother had that now familiar secret smile on her face: she had opened my room up again for Sean to deliver another surprise. There in my room, placed on my pillows and hugging a lacy red heart, sat a six-foot black and white panda.

Sean continued his courtship. By Christmas break, as a sweet and balanced love grew within me, I agreed to marry Sean, but not until the following year when I came back from summer vacation. I was only twenty years old and was quite sure that my parents would not agree with this whirlwind courtship. In August of '73, I would be twenty-one and free to marry.

Sean asked me not to go back to Chicago for the summer but to move in with him. We discussed the pros and cons, yet we still had not come up with a plan. Then around February of '73, he began to talk about something else. Several times in those last few months, Sean shared that he had started to have odd dreams and a funny sense, a premonition that he was going to die that summer. He felt that if I stayed in Albuquerque, he would survive whatever was coming, but if we separated, he would never see me again. These feelings concerned him.

We had often talked about my teachers, my intuitive gifts, and the work I did with them. I was confident I would be able to sense anything that serious in his life. I asked both my teachers, yet neither one could detect anything negative. I meditated on this often and found nothing untoward in his field, so I thought he was mistaken. Sean and I concluded it must be his sorrow brought on by my departure. I knew him well enough to know he was frank. An honest man, he merely spoke his truth.

After weeks of deliberation, I finally agreed to stay in Albuquerque for the summer. Towards the end of the semester, I moved most of my things from my dorm room into his house. Then suddenly I changed my mind. There was no particular reason; restlessness flooded through me at the thought of remaining in Albuquerque, so I bought a ticket home.

On 29 May, he drove me to the airport. Sean restated his fears of never seeing me again. At the gate, I kissed the tip of his nose. "Please don't worry! Nothing's going to happen to you, except I'll get to rub your nose in your words when you pick me up in August."

We kissed one last time, and he gave me a long, tender, can't-let-go hug. I had found a 45 rpm record of the song "Leaving on a Jet Plane" by Peter, Paul, and Mary. The aching lyrics as she departs and the promise of marriage upon her return struck a chord, so I tried to tuck the little black disc into his jacket pocket during the hug. It was too big. He looked at it, sighed, and hugged me one more time. I turned and waved before I entered the plane.

On 3 June, Sean called. I was working two jobs and rarely home, so it was close to midnight when the phone rang, which upset the entire household. He begged me to return and once more mentioned that he felt he would never see me again. Tired and angry that he had called so late, I refused and tried to get off the phone. I told him we could talk about it another day. He would not say goodbye this time: he would not hang up. Exasperated, I slammed the phone down.

The next day I felt terrible about our fight, especially how it had ended. It was not like us to have fractious words. I was not sure when we would talk again, so I wrote him a letter. A possible compromise had popped into my mind. Instead of returning at the end of August, I offered to come back in the second week in July, halfway through the vacation. I mailed the letter later that day, but he never received it. We never spoke again. The following day he died in a car accident.

Losing him was devastating. His premonitions haunted me. Was it true? Would he have survived if I had stayed? The way I hung up played over again and again in my mind.

I returned to Albuquerque at the end of August. Since March 1973, I had only worked with Bonnie. Our classes revolved around in-depth astrology. Shortly after my arrival, I went to see her. She had heard nothing of the tragedy. When she opened the door, she stopped with a surprised look on her face. Instead of the warm hugs I usually received, she asked, "Lesley! What's happened?"

She led me into the kitchen and sat me down. I choked up and could not speak. She offered to make us both some tea. Numerous bags of Celestial Seasonings littered the table. I picked Red Zinger. After a couple of sips, Bonnie remarked on my shattered aura. Then she asked me what had happened to me over the summer. I burst into tears.

We talked for almost five hours that day. At first, I acted surly. I wanted to know why she had not seen what was coming when it was to be such a tragedy. She tried to help me understand that the future isn't carved in stone; therefore, it is not "predictable." The human mind and the immortal soul will have different agendas. Sean had to go; he had to return. For whatever reason, my soul chose to stay.

By then it had dawned on me that if I had stayed, I would have been seated right next to him on that fateful night. Several of our friends were carpooling to a concert and, because Sean had a van, he always drove the extra people.

I resented what I considered a tidy explanation, feeling that somehow, one of us should have seen what was coming and been able to avoid this catastrophe. I, we, did not protect Sean. On the other hand, I would go on the attack, maybe I had not been trained well enough.

As much as I wanted to discount what Bonnie said, by the end of our visit, I could not. I agreed to continue weekly astrology classes with her, but, by the end of October, bitterness had seeped in and shut down any enthusiasm for life, liberty, and the pursuit of happiness within me. I stopped my metaphysical studies.

As a Psych major, I understood the power of suggestion, which led me to doubt all the years of training, all the shamans and medicine people I had met, all the miraculous things I had witnessed. Ultimately, I considered it all a bunch of rubbish. By the end of that year, I firmly rooted myself in the realm of materialist science and atheism.

Once again, I turned off my intuitive channel.

With Roberta Flack's words ringing in my ears, I sat at my desk for over an hour as the slideshow took me throughout our life together, his death, and the aftermath. The memories, which flooded through me, were both delightful and miserable, but, instead of happening fifteen years earlier with all the subsequent levels of healing I had lived through in between, I experienced the raw pain as if all of it, the good and the bad, had happened that morning.

The realization that Sean had been the light being from my core soul group shook me. As much as I consciously remembered all the talks, the walks, and the beauty of Upstairs, I hadn't connected the dots when Meena referred to a light being with whom I had signed up to incarnate, help out, die young, and go back. Finally, his premonitions made sense to me. They surfaced from his subconscious understanding of our contract.

I went home and told Beatriz she could leave early. I cuddled with my children, read to them, and took a nap. I took time off for the next two days. The roller coaster had cast me out at the top, and I needed a sabbatical. My children and I snuggled up to read or watch movies, but when they were napping or eating, and Beatriz was there, I journaled and journaled and journaled again. I could no longer ignore the split between my spirituality and my humanity. Atheism no longer worked for me. I decided to go back and immerse myself in what I knew before, in what I studied in Albuquerque: i.e., the beautiful awareness of opening up my intuitive, spiritual channel.

I decided that I wanted to extend my time off. Following an impulse, I went to a travel agent and got a catalog of summer cottages in England. I looked at summer cottages all over England and Ireland, calling dozens of possible places to rent. I thought it unlikely that I would find anything available at that late date but I had to try. I wanted to be far away and in a foreign place, a place that I could enjoy traveling and leave behind the distractions brought on by all the daily demands of my job.

However, the following week, by some synchronistic fluke, there had been a cancellation an hour before they received my inquiry and I found a summer cottage to rent for five weeks. By the end of June, I packed up my stepdaughter, my two children, and Beatriz. We traveled to a small country cottage on a large estate near Gloucester, England.

We spent the next few weeks traveling the countryside, visiting castles, a butterfly farm, and countless small towns. I would take my stepdaughter to London once a week to the theater or the museums and leave the little ones with Beatriz. Sometimes I would drop Beatriz and Cara off somewhere and go home with my babies. We also tracked down anything having to do with King Arthur, from Tintagel to the Tor to Camelot.

I found bookstores in every town and selected spiritually based books. I was browsing in a second-hand store when a copy of the Bhagavad Gita, the book that had fallen off a shelf in my high school library and snapped me out of atheism, dropped yet again. I did not buy the book, but I did purchase a copy of the Upanishads, a translation of Rumi's poetry, and books about Brigit of Kildare and Hildegard of Bingen.

I meditated daily and settled down into an earth rhythm, quite easy to do while on a contemplative vacation in the spiritually charged parts of western England. Instead of falling asleep with my memories of Upstairs, I wrote about them in a journal. Often while meditating, I would hear the faint chanting or the glass chimes.

After my NDE, I began to have a series of extraordinary dreams that I kept in a separate dream journal. Some were fun, others educational. There was always the dream-like, fuzzy quality about them, which dissipated, like the morning fog, minutes after I would open my eyes. I began to train myself to write immediately, even when I was half-awake.

Then one night, while I slept, an extraordinary thing happened. Instead of the funny, foggy processes that I entertained myself with at night, when I fell asleep I visited my soul group Upstairs, a dream that was so ultra-real I knew it was not a dream. It opened with my arrival in the oak forest. I floated down from above and landed right next to the stream. Nothing had changed except that only four light beings sat at the table. Teemo sat with Meena and two other women.

I half ran, half stumbled over to them and plopped down in my seat. I lay my head down on the table and laughed and cried as I announced that life on earth was exhausting. Meena said that they had cautioned me about how difficult it would be at first.

"Yes, but it is so much harder than I thought!" Meena rubbed my back, and we laughed again.

"Remember when I said a few years wouldn't be a big deal?" I asked as I raised my head. "Does everyone run into the same problems?"

I did not hear the answer to my question. The vision faded away, and our talk turned into murmurings. I jolted awake, the dream burned into my brain. Instead of the foggy fumbling for paper and pen, I sat upright, feeling the same open joy that I had experienced Upstairs; every single detail easy to remember. From that point on, I began to bring up the memories of my journey before, lovingly kept to the side until I could face them again.

One day we piled in the car for a day trip to visit Stonehenge and Salisbury. Stonehenge was extraordinary. The beauty of the plains, the tremendous not-so-silent stones with the breezes whistling around the corners and the circular mounds, all combined to produce a peaceful state as I walked along.

We left to go to Salisbury for lunch and sightseeing. As we got closer to our destination, a hill on my right caught my attention. I felt a sharp drumming beat in my body. There was no signage, yet I felt an intense, instinctive pull towards it. I shook my head and thought I must have been imagining things.

We had a lovely lunch, walked around and took some photos. As we drove back home, we took the same road. As we approached the hill, I began to feel the same drumming again, but this time, a sign stated that the ruins were of Old Sarum, the site of the earliest settlement in Wiltshire. I laughed as I realized my intuition was full on now. I promised myself to stay objective to any instinctive insights, but never to completely doubt it again.

After I returned in July, transcendent "aha" synchronicities rained down all around me. Peeling off the materialist armor that I had wrapped around myself for the past fifteen years, I allowed the dance of the Divine to play out every day.

New people that lived contemplative lifestyles continued to cross my path. Tanque Verde Ranch's new horse vet, LuAnn G., added a holistic aspect to her veterinary business. As we developed a friendship, she introduced me to many of her other spiritual friends.

Not long after that, as I walked down to the Tack Room to check on a schedule change, I noticed a young woman, Dana P., standing by the gate. She looked lost. All the cowboys were out on rides. She held a beautifully framed painting. Since Tanque Verde Ranch proper was open only to registered guests, I walked over and asked if I could help her. She had created an intricate bead and saguaro rib frame for a client who happened to be one of our employees. The cowgirl who ordered it told her to drop it off at the Tack Room, but, by the time Dana finished the order, the person no longer worked for us. I offered to get her the employee's contact information.

As she recalls, the next sentence out of my mouth surprised her. I asked her if she knew how to ride. She said yes, so I invited her to go on a horseback ride with me. There was something about her that made me feel comfortable. Dana was relaxed and earthy, pragmatic and cosmic at the same time. The way we talked reminded me of my days in Albuquerque. That began a life-long friendship.

We went riding the next day and, afterward, Dana pulled out a deck of tarot cards and asked if I wanted to have a reading as a thank you. At that point, I had not shared my history with her. I quietly shuffled the cards several times, not knowing what to expect. I had not touched tarot cards in fifteen years. So many memories poured in that I fought back my tears as we continued.

Dana bases her card layout on the twelve houses of astrology. She laid down three circles, one for the past, one for the present, and one for the future. The three rings also integrated the body, mind, and soul connections.

At the outset, something Dana said gave me chills. After studying the cards for a minute or two, she looked up at me and asked, "Why did you turn your light off?"

I froze. What was it about those words? Another door opened, and more memories slipped in at the words that had echoed in my life so many years ago. She continued with the reading and hit many of the highs and lows of my life. We talked for another hour as I opened up. For the first time since my accident, I could speak with someone about the sacred implications, someone who had a strong spiritual foundation that enabled her to understand what I had experienced. We talked about the entire journey without questions or ridicule.

The best part was the way she used her insights and her intuition to inform and inspire me, to encourage me to work on bettering myself. Instead of portraying a fatalistic view of my life, Dana had a knack for showing me ways to uplift and smooth out the bumps. She recommended many books to read and workshops to take from gifted teachers. I began to branch out on my spiritual path.

We both wound up taking Neuro-Linguistics Programming (NLP) classes and practiced the techniques on the odd days we saw each other.

Meena's idea to dust off my BA in Psych was coming to fruition. I also took different art classes like jewelry making and watercolor painting to connect with my inner artist.

Before my head injury, our marriage had troubles. We were at the point of seeking counsel when I got hurt. With no memory of the past, life seemed like a clean slate. While I scrambled to get back into my roles as a wife, as a mother, and as the VP of Operations, we put our problems on hold. However, by the beginning of 1991, the difficulties that brought us to counseling caused the marriage to decline and ultimately end.

During the first week of June 1991, I moved off the ranch into Tucson proper. Even though I was only fifteen miles from the guest ranch, it seemed as if I had moved to a brand new city. My entire life—my friends, my social life, and my career—stayed behind. I had two small children, aged four and six, and I needed to figure out what to do with the rest of my life.

In the beginning, I had to manage all the human dramas: developing new friendships, building a new career, forming a client base, learning how to be a single mom, and even dating again. I opened a business as an interior design consultant while I finished my studies in NLP and Hypnotherapy. At the same time, I still used Tarot cards, bringing the archetypal pictures into the sessions. My clientele built up by word-of-mouth.

The more profound my spiritual awareness grew, the more I felt the rift between it and my day-to-day life. I could sit deep in the bliss of meditation. However, when I finished and had to do the work of daily life, it vanished. I had two distinctly different parts inside. It became abundantly clear that, to balance myself, I had to introduce them to each other and figure out a way to integrate the routine, multi-tasking reflexes of my human mind with my inner divinity, my immortal soul. My two parts would have to work as a team. I did not want one side to dominate and always lead the other.

To that end, I decided to pursue two paths: one as a student of the spirit again, and the other, the road of a contemplative. To begin with, I visited different energy healers. I wanted to use Reiki and Jin Shin Jyutsu to clear my cobwebs. I felt as if I were a novice, caught up in the jumble of recreating my perception of Self. Therefore, I assumed that all the spiritual teachers could see me better than I could see myself. I gave away my power, my sense of authority. By trial and error, I learned to differentiate between those who perceived me and those who were projecting their lessons onto me.

Decades before, when I began my spiritual lessons in Albuquerque, none of my teachers would explain to me what any symbols or dreams meant. Instead, they insisted that I knew the answers deep within and guided me on how to unravel *my* interpretations. At that time, I was a typical eighteen-year-old. My impatience bubbled up. I wanted the answers right away, so sometimes I resented their teaching style.

For example, Bonnie had taught me to use the archetypal images on the individual Tarot cards to gain insights into the core of my intuition. To make this point during our first lesson, she pulled out the Knight of Cups. In the picture, a knight sits upon a white steed offering a golden cup to someone we cannot see. Pointing to the scene, she asked, "Let's talk about one aspect of this picture. What would a horse symbolize to you?"

"I love them," I answered. "Horses are affectionate and bond with us like big dogs. Life would be easier. I could travel much further than walking by myself. For me, the horse represents an elevation of my life or a journey in some way or another. And, as you suggested, if I consider what the horse meant in the 1300s when artists first painted these cards, it is a sign of wealth and stability. It would indicate a turn of events that represents more freedom or more travel."

"Not for me!" She laughed as she said, "When I see a knight I interpret it as a warning. I hate horses! Scary, smelly beasts. Too big and too strong, they can seriously hurt you. You can never tell what they are going to do. When I see a horse on a tarot card, I take that as a sign that something's wrong. I must slow down to the point that I can watch the situation, and anyone else involved, a lot more carefully. If I only told you what the horse symbolized, in truth, I would be telling you what the horse meant *to me*. You have to meditate on your intuitive self, your connection to God, and realize what each image or symbol means *to you*. Even though our translations are opposite each other, both versions are correct because the picture on the tarot card is simply a tool to aid us in understanding our inner realm and what our guides tell us at that level."

That style of teaching helped me to see the motivation of anyone who jumped in to help me now. Some guided with a teacher's touch; others tried to squeeze me into their self-constructed paradigm. Eventually, I could tell the difference and settled into working with another healer, Jana K. She became my Reiki teacher. Over the next two years, I became a certified Reiki Master in three modalities with her: Usui, Shamballa, and Angelic Reiki.

My friendship with Dana P. continued. We met regularly to discuss different levels of consciousness and all the subsequent mysteries. From time to time, we would touch upon several components of my NDE in a piece-meal fashion. I was experiencing tremendous personal and spiritual growth, so the tiny minutia was not relevant at that time. Things that related to our inner, or transcendent, quests took center stage, so details about Upstairs, the buildings, the waterfalls, even some of the other light beings were not as important as the discussions I had with Meena and Ra-u or lessons I brought back, both to teach and to learn. We would talk, meditate, and then share insights. Dana had such a vibrant, yet free, capability not only grasping any situation, but she could also explain her discoveries and epiphanies in simple ways that were easy to assimilate.

One day we explored the significance of the blindfolded Bodhisattvas having their personal spiritual growth obscured before incarnating into younger soul families to facilitate growth. I decided to call these volunteers Houdini Kids after Houdini himself. I recalled a film I had seen in which he had been blindfolded, tied up, and put into a bag before being thrown into the ocean. He had to do all the work by himself to get out. It seemed to reflect what we had to do: give up our spiritual memory and find our inner light all by ourselves.

In some of these families, Houdini Kids had been exposed to abusive and hate-filled ideas and lifestyles. How might the act of incarnating blindfolded work? Or worse, what if they all failed? The only way it could work would be for the Houdini Kids to feel that there was something bigger and better than what they found around them. Even the wealthy kids would feel a yearning that their lifestyle did not fulfill. They would locate the courage to go against the grain, to go against the conditioning, and find their inner connection to the Divine.

How was that to happen? I had the outline of what I had been shown Upstairs, the fact that many old souls were now coming down blindfolded to their heritage and helping to awaken global consciousness by digging deep within. However, the nuts and bolts of how it worked had not been shown to me.

In my meditation, after I asked for more clarification. I experienced a particularly strong vision of how it worked. The vision started with my dropping down to earth as a light being in an entirely opalescent body. As the vision unfolded, my soul group narrated what these allegorical images represented.

A multitude of volunteers had agreed to erase their sense of right and wrong, erase their deep-seated spiritual wisdom, and erase their history. Placed in families in which there would be no mention of higher consciousness, they had to seek another pathway. They came down to help facilitate growth in forgiveness, for what did the people on earth need more after all the deaths in the world wars but to forgive? They landed in the depth of human fight/flight/freeze responses, ranging from healthy families of younger souls that did not think outside the box to relatives that lived lives of pure irresponsibility or cruelty. Even all the way to family units steeped in immorality and corruption.

I saw my body splash into a murky swamp. Several others landed one by one with at least several hundred feet up to a mile or two between them; all consciously spaced in different directions. Oh, I thought, this is what I had been doing Upstairs: placing the volunteers. Of course, it follows that I would follow their example.

The volunteers knew they had to extricate themselves from any fear-based, divisive programming all by themselves. However, after incarnating, they had no memory of that pledge. Even though they would eventually resist what they witnessed in their culture, their families, or their schools, they had to find their inner light within all by themselves, and keep what good they absorbed by filtering out fear-based thinking. As they grew, they dropped the competitive herd reflexes to a cooperative mindset.

I walked over and saw my human body wholly submerged in the sludge, the skin had lost the light and had turned into my human skin. I struggled to lift one finger above the waterline. As I did, it turned back to the opalescent body, and the mire lessened. By living and forgiving, I began to soak up the dank water around me.

Some volunteers did not make it, having landed in an utterly hostile, environment. They sank shortly after incarnating.

Over to my right, another light being struggled and finally sank to the bottom. Almost immediately, another light being landed and absorbed whatever essence had been left behind.

As more emerged, the momentum shifted but the last part, the sticking to your guns in the face of the majority point of view, was the hardest part.

As I climbed out, the ground grew more firm. It became more difficult to get my lower legs and feet from the bog. I strained to free my ankles and finally pulled myself away from the densely packed earth. I stood up, and bright green grass grew as far as I could see on the ground that now stretched around me. Miniscule star-shaped white and pale yellow flowers stretched out in every direction. Others around me struggled to remove themselves with varying degrees of success. Some had popped out before me; some were stuck halfway out.

Everyone's struggles paved the way for another level of light beings: a newer group that could land and keep their light within on the surface. The more pure light these Bodhisattvas brought to the shade, the more additional Bodhisattvas could arrive, and it would spark a global awareness of the fact that we are all One.

Faint laughter reached my ears. I looked above and saw an endless group of other translucent light beings landing, yet they kept their brightness as they hit the ground running. This new group of Bodhisattvas incarnated to boost another grouping of collaborative living, a group in which children under the age of twenty would be the next wave of innovators and spiritual leaders.

Drawn back to contemplative traditions, India beckoned. During the summer months when my children traveled with their father, I would go to ashrams, either in the States or abroad. I started at Sai Baba's ashram in Puttaparthi, India, and Mother Meera's ashram in Schaumburg, Germany for two to three weeks at a time. I also attended Sri Ammachi's and Sri Karunamayi's retreats throughout the United States. Stilling the "monkey mind" became my priority. Pathways opened for my inner self to receive insights from my soul group Upstairs. I had a series of extraordinary experiences and visions. Gradually, the partition shrank between my immortal Self and my human self. I knew my goal of integration was attainable; minutes stretched into hours that then extended into days when my humanity and my divinity were in perfect harmony. The more I practiced, the longer the light remained.

On my first night home after a particularly wonderful trip to India, I had another dream in which I visited Upstairs. I walked through the doorway into one of the smaller rooms. Ra-u sat at a table conversing with another man whom I did not recognize. They both looked startled as I walked in, then they both laughed. Ra-u said he did not realize I could visit and then asked how he might help.

I wanted to see what I looked like Upstairs. Both men smiled. Ra-u took me into another room with a gold-framed mirror on one wall. I looked at myself. Pale golden freckles sprinkled over my heart-shaped face. My chin-length hair formed large golden brown curls, and I had bright turquoise eyes.

"Oh my gosh! I look like such a kid!" I smiled as I played with a curl.

"What do you think? That we all look young and you don't?" Ra-u said.

After that, I woke up.

One question continued to puzzle me: how does one jump one's contract? Nothing I had ever read suggested an answer. Nor were any of my teachers or friends able to offer me any definitive answers. They theorized, yet none of their suppositions rang true.

During my next trip to Puttaparthi, I decided to ask within for guidance about overriding an agreement. I wanted to know the details; maybe not why, but at least how. I did not waver in my intention.

In Sai Baba's Puttaparthi mandir, or temple, there is an Omkar meditation every morning at 4:30 am, so I set my alarm. I woke up to find the ashram's generator had died and my room was pitch-black. After a quick splash of icy water to wake me up, and a fumble through the different suitcases to find the appropriate clothing, I could only hope that everything was at least color-coordinated. Somehow tying up a sari was second nature to me. I hurried down the stairs and followed the crowds of people walking toward the mandir. We sat down and the temple Brahmin, or priest, began the chant. The voices of several thousand people joined in as we all repeated OM, over and over again, in perfect unison.

My entire body reverberated with the sound. I slipped deeper and deeper into a meditative state. As I floated in this bliss, I had a powerful insight.

I had a vision of Sean and me. We held hands and floated above the earth, looking down at the countries and oceans. About four to five months before Sean and I were to have the accident, a magnetic force gently began to pull at our immortal souls. Hundreds of phosphorous yellow, green and blue threads connected us to our lives; threads as thin as a spider's silk. We turned away from the earth and, as we floated away, one by one, individual threads began to snap.

A glistening pathway formed ahead of us, resembling the spattering of light that reflects on the sea when the sun dips to the horizon. At that point, the energy flow became stronger. Sean and I held hands and smiled at each other as we continued to drift away. The magnetic draw continued to detach us from our lives. We knew what was happening and we accepted it. Any attachment to our survival instincts dissolved so that we could make this transition.

As the timeline in the vision fast-forwarded a couple of months, the flow's pull increased but, for some reason, I became restless. I kept glancing over my shoulder and looking behind. Even though we still held hands, I lingered as Sean drifted a foot ahead. The magnetic current grew even stronger and became bumpy.

A few weeks later, the magnetic force intensified to the point of no return. By now, we drifted along a couple of feet apart from each other. We stretched to keep our fingertips touching. As Sean entered the denser energy force, I let go and abruptly broke away. I was intent on returning to earth.

I paused and watched Sean. He looked back, smiling but puzzled. He had already entered the energy field and swept away.

The vision faded. It had exhausted me; spent, I collapsed. When I came to, I lay on the ground. I was alone in the Darshan hall except for a Seva Dal, one of the women who helped at the ashram. During my vision, I had unconsciously wept, so she sat next to me, singing bhajans and rubbing my back.

When I had the strength to sit up, she smiled kindly and handed me sweet upma, holy Prasad, a treat made from creamed wheat. She said Sai Baba had stopped by and materialized vibhuti, sacred ash, for me, which she held in her cupped right hand. She rubbed it all over my forehead and arms. He had instructed her to stay with me until I returned from "far away."

She called me "Missy" and led me through all the twists and turns of the ashram until we found my room. We had many stops and starts as I became exhausted after a few steps. I felt like a truck had run over me yet this was a significant turning point for me.

From the insights that I received in England to my visions during the time in India, the individual pieces of my puzzle of integrating my immortal soul with my human life came into focus. Now all I had to do was put them all together.

Back in Tucson, I made a point of organizing my thoughts. I journaled, meditated, and then journaled again. Several times, I channeled different exercises with help from my soul group Upstairs. These not only firmly grounded my connections to them but also formed the foundation for a self-empowering workshop that I then taught to my clients.

One of the most profound lessons came to me late one summer day. I was still stuck in juggling all the multi-tasking parts of human life while my connection to the Divine seemed to slip away. It completely disengaged and hovered a short distance away, just out of reach. In my meditations, I could visit my well of perpetual hope, but I could not stay. Then one day, the tools for the solution appeared.

The format I used for meditation was standard: sit still, close my eyes, shut out the world, and quiet the mind. To stay centered while I was busy with the daily routines, I developed a movement meditation by turning my everyday chores into tools to elevate mindfulness.

For at least one hour a day, I remained focused on my chore. Usually, I would do two things at once, such as watching television as I did repetitive, tedious tasks like ironing. Now I would stay focused on the fabric, on the steam, on the artistry of the pattern, or in the game of seeking out the wrinkles. It was just for an hour after which I would click on the music, the television, or call someone.

With that slight adjustment, within a couple of weeks, I sensed a profound, abiding serenity while I actively completed routine chores such as chopping vegetables, washing dishes, or gardening. Just for an hour. I could remain in that sweet spot, that inner light where patience and peace vibrated from every one of my cells. When I developed this ability for task-oriented movement meditation, it became easier for me to receive help from my soul group. Several times I had visions that triggered an *aha* moment, so I would write them down. One exercise that finally integrated my humanity with my Divinity I named *Take Off the Mantles*.

Late one summer afternoon, I sat by my pond. Determined to integrate my human and spiritual parts into a cohesive "oneness," I stilled my mind. Up to that point, I still felt like a circus act standing on the backs of two separate horses. The trick was not only to keep my balance; the animals must work in unison. To integrate my immortal soul with my fight/flight/freeze reflex would elevate my humanness instead of having to put my inner light over on the back burner anytime I started with my housework.

Soon, in my mind's eye, I could see tiny lights spiraling around everything before they streamed off in different directions. With the light trails dancing in the background, Meena and Ra-u appeared. Experiencing a constant connection with selfless love still eluded me. Could I stay in touch with the Divine, twenty-four seven? Or at least nip back in when life on earth knocked me off the rails.

Ra-u told me to keep my focus on the whole instead of being sidetracked by the parts. The real whole, my authentic Self, encompassed *all of me* as a unified field. In my daily life, I would identify only with the wrappings of my life, not my spark of Divinity. The roles I played defined me. I did not have to give up those functions or responsibilities; in fact, I could not. What these new volunteers were accomplishing was raising consciousness to the point that no one needed to forsake the material world and hide in a cave or convent to maintain their spiritual journey. The simple lesson would connect me to both the spiritual and material world.

I sat very still. My magnetic field came into view. Layers upon layers of rainbow colors encircled me: colors that twisted and turned as they streamed from me. It resembled a 3-D kaleidoscope.

It was time for me to see what layers had originated in my magnetic energy, in my connection to that indescribable Divine energy field.

Meena asked me to let go of the wrappers and introduce myself to my core, my immortal soul from which the entire energy field originated. To do this, she told me to think of each part of my life, each role, position, or responsibility that kept me busy and made me who I was right now. The first one I thought of was a *mother*. Meena smiled and said she would remove that "wrapper." An arrangement of light lines peeled off my body and formed a pattern that resembled a shimmering multi-color kaleidoscope. It unfolded around me like a Hoberman collapsible sphere.

She asked, "What's the next role?" *Daughter* popped into mind, and the next pattern peeled off me causing the first separate sphere to grow larger. One by one, additional positions peeled off: *sister, divorcee, interior designer, chess teacher, therapist, farmer, jeweler,* and so on. The more functions I named, the more levels of my identity emerged and hovered in the air. Eventually, I was surrounded by more than twenty concentric geodesic domes. All of them were made up of spectacular, yet completely different, patterns.

At the same time, as every role left, a pathway opened for the light within to brighten and grow stronger. My tasks streamed out through the area of my second and third chakras, and, as they did, my fingers, toes, and scalp glowed. The more roles I released, the more the human form trickled away. What remained was my outline in opalescent light, so bright that I could not see any details of my hands or clothing.

I stood in an entirely different light body than I had experienced Upstairs. All my roles, reduced to wrappings, rotated around me. I felt them distinctly separate from my core.

"Don't forget the last role. Let go of being human. What is left is your immortal soul. The roles everyone plays here on earth are critical and significant, yet, if you become too attached to the different parts, you'll forget who you really are." Meena's voice came from somewhere. At that moment, all I could see was pure light and colorful patterns of energy flowing through me.

The vision stayed for a long time before it gently faded away. When it ended, something within me had transformed. Initially, all the roles I played fused onto me like a hide; a covering. Our skin is made up of multiple layers of tissue that guards our internal parts: our muscles, ligaments, and organs. In addition, like skin, my fused roles had become stable but impermeable. It may have shielded me, but it also blocked me. I only glimpsed my true Self, my immortal soul, from time to time: the essential part of me who endured the stampede and viewed the reality of the universe.

I dashed into the house to write it all down. I wanted to develop an exercise to anchor the lesson. It became a helpful tool to use whenever I felt cut off from my immortal soul again.

I made a list of all the roles, functions, responsibilities, and relationships that I had at that time. Then I ranked them from one to twenty-three. Number one represented my human form. Number two was my favorite role; twenty-three indicated my least favorite. I cut each digit into separate pieces of paper and popped them into a cobalt blue velvet bag. I also got the idea to add some little items that symbolized a particular role, such as photos of my children or a chess piece of the queen. For some of the descriptions, I sketched a symbol of the function on that piece of paper.

I had been seated during my meditation. I knew that, if pressed for space, I could do it that way again. However, I decided to add movement too. In my backyard, I paced off 100 feet. I placed a chair in one spot, walked back fifty feet, and placed a big rock down to signify the halfway mark. Back at the starting point, I poured out all the items from my velvet bag onto a small tray and sorted out the slips of paper. I placed the largest number on top, with the others descending to number one.

I faced the chair, took a deep breath and said, "I completely release my role as teacher; I give teaching back to the universe. My immortal soul steps forward." With every step I took, I put a slip of paper or the symbolic object on the ground. I made sure to pace myself, so I could place all the slips down before I came to the halfway mark. At number one, I put a photo of myself for the role I play of being a human being and said, "I completely release my mortality, my human body. I am my immortal soul."

By the time I had put down this last piece of paper, I was slightly unnerved. I felt naked at the same time that I felt complete bliss. Two emotions tried to dominate at the same time: fear and love. Love eventually tipped me over, and I merged with the light—there was nothing on me, and nothing inside of me—selfless love glowed from head to toe. My immortal soul walked to the chair and sat down to savor this new mode of perception. For about fifteen minutes, my mind completely converged with my eternal soul.

To complete the meditation and thoroughly transfer it into my consciousness, I strolled back down the path towards the starting point. I reclaimed my roles, but, as I lifted up every piece of paper, I said, "My immortal soul chooses to be human, too. My immortal soul chooses to be a mother, too." I repeated an affirmation for each of the papers, all the way to the end. One by one, I retrieved all the mantles I had taken off. An incredible awareness filled my mind. These images no longer merged into my identity. Instead of my being fused to my roles, my characters, they now rested on me like clothing. They were removable. They stayed on me as light as a silk robe. My two parts had finally merged.

I went to a dictionary and researched the word *role*. I found out that, initially, it came from the theater, from the Old French, and it means *having the sense of a part one has to play*. As I had grown up, I created inner, subconscious dictionary definitions of each of my roles that reflected my history, both cultural and experiential. I had played many roles in my life. These characters had become so ingrained in my psyche that they defined not only who I was, but also who I could be in the future. Thanks to my new awareness, my roles would be beautiful mantles that I could choose to put on. They no longer could act as barricades in my life.

Before practicing this new meditation, if I attached too much importance to a role, I had a difficult time when any changes occurred. Now during regular cycles of transition, my perspective would be elevated. For example, if I only identify myself as being a mother, what do I do when my children leave home? I am primarily who I am, an immortal soul, while I can also participate in the role of mothering. However, it is what I *do*, and I can choose to do many things, while always being who I *am*, an immortal soul.

I had come to call my inner light my *well of perpetual hope*. I knew that if ever I became derailed, as happens in life, I could pull out my hope-filled bag and repeat this meditation. Every time I reconnect with that refreshing light, I am back on track within minutes, not weeks and months like before.

By 1996, I had established a strong client base for the workshops and the individual follow-up sessions. I had one client in particular, Kathy P., who traveled all around the country. She had introduced me to some friends of hers in Los Angeles, and some of them attended my workshops. One of my L.A. clients, Michelle L., often went to the Canyon Ranch Resort. I did not know much about it other than that they used to bring out their guests for unique breakfast rides at the Tanque Verde Ranch. At the time, I thought Canyon Ranch was just a fancy gym.

One day Michelle called me from Canyon Ranch to let me know that their resident tarot reader had recently left. She had mentioned my name and, with her recommendation, asked me if I would be interested in coming over for an interview.

I told her I was busy, but I would consider it. I did not realize they had metaphysical providers there. Later that day I lunched with a friend, Molly T., whose son attended my chess class. She worked in the fitness department at Canyon Ranch and encouraged me to try it. Molly knew of my Intuitive Therapist career. That was in September of '96. I went over to have lunch with Michelle and an interview. They hired me on the spot, so I started the following month.

The day before I started my job at Canyon Ranch was the third time I visited my soul group Upstairs. In my dream, Meena and I walked into the Hall of Records. We sat down in two chairs in the center of the main room. Two cups of what looked like tea sat on a small table between the chairs. It was the only time I had ever seen refreshments Upstairs. We sipped it as we chatted.

Meena stated how much I would enjoy my work at Canyon Ranch, both because of the work I would be doing and the people that I would meet. Here was the place she had mentioned as we decided if I stayed or not: a healing center where many other light beings already worked. Many of my clientele would also be the light beings who had volunteered to come down blindfolded. We continued our conversation as this dream faded out. After I awoke, I snuggled deeper into my covers and thanked the Divine for these dreams that had started since I returned. Even though I had remembered many of them, the quality and joy that seeped into the vast majority of them, now, was something for which I was always thankful.

As I drove to Canyon Ranch, the day had dawned bright and beautiful. What a way to start a new job! The energy vortexes that spun all around the property made me giddy. I noted that the property had been well chosen for a body/mind/spirit destination.

I parked in the employee parking lot and walked over to my office. Since the tarot reader before me had only worked part-time, I had been set up in a spare room tucked away near the fitness department. They had given me a recorder and several blank tapes. I brought along three of my different decks. I sat down, closed my eyes, and made a simple promise to the Divine. "I came back to help, and help I will. If I can make a difference in the life of one person, if I can give them the tools to find that peaceful place within, then anyone else I help will be icing on the cake."

My first client had signed up for a reading on a whim yet was having second thoughts. John T. stood in the doorway and talked to me from there. He hesitated because he thought it might be like in the movies. He would pull the Death card, and his life would be downhill from there.

We chatted while I explained to him that the pictures were allegorical, not literal and that no one could predict when anybody might die. Anyway, the archetypal interpretation of that card signified transformation. Death held a banner with a white rose, which symbolized spiritual purity. Just as a caterpillar has to "die" to become a butterfly, there will be many times in our lives when we would outgrow something, and we would let it go.

We talked about many different cultures that use the butterfly to symbolize rebirth, new growth, new opportunities, or a second chance. He stood in the doorway, still skittish but laughing as we talked.

Eventually, he came in and sat down. Since I did not have any clients after him, I added a bit more to the session. Happily, he survived the reading, and we went on to have many more meetings as well as a friendship that grew over time. Many years later, he talked the skeptical Leslie Klein into coming in for reading; the man who would eventually inspire and facilitate me to stay on point and write this book.

And so the circle completes itself and starts anew.

"After your death, you will be what you were before your birth. There is not a grain of dust, not an atom that can become nothing, yet man believes that death is the annihilation of his being."

~ *Arthur Schopenhauer*

Chapter Five

A Dialogue on Life and Death:

A candid conversation between Lesley and Leslie Klein

As Leslie Klein asked me the thought-provoking questions that added the details to my experience, he asked many other particulars about other subjects relating to things I learned after I returned. These are topics that I chose not to add to the above text because they were about themes different from my experience Upstairs. Leslie's questions brought out other diverse spiritual points that I include in the next chapter. I retained the chitchat structure that emerged from our sessions.

Until I sat down to write the book, I had never put my NDE in any linear order. Previously, every night as I started to fall asleep, I would remember different parts of my journey Upstairs. I would focus only on a particular scene or two: my time in the Hall of Records, for example, or the various discussions with the light beings. Most of the time, I would focus on my first arrival: the sense of awe I experienced as I felt that all-enveloping feeling of love. Other times, I would recall the time that I looked up and saw the Unmanifest over my head and the intensity of the love and adoration that I felt.

When Leslie Klein was asking me all those questions, I was able to link them up in a line. In addition, many more details of the journey opened up, such as when I was looking in the river and tried to figure out what was swimming in the river, or going across the meadow with the plethora of birds and flowers.

My answers reflect impressions and the information I have received after my near-death experience. Please remember that these are my thoughts and, in some cases, my conjectures. When I speak, it is from my experience so I will not be saying, In My Humble Opinion before each and every question. This is my realm, the reflection of earth at its finest. Other realms may be a spark of consciousness flowing into nothing. As I mentioned, there were many other realms surrounding mine and we seem to have the freedom, and the inclination, to flow into many of them. I have bumped into people who believe in broad-based sweeping generalizations such as all psychics have an NDE in their history all the way to the belief that a realm that reflects earth exists because you form what is familiar. I even have that as one of my jobs; however, I formed or staged something very personal from their history and the world I went to was nothing like I had ever experienced here on earth.

To quote Krishnamurti: "The ability to observe without evaluating is the highest form of intelligence." Therefore, as you read this chapter, if the images resonate with you, that is lovely. They also may be close to something you know at a deep level and the thoughts help you to bring your inner voice up to your own awareness. If not, no problem. There are many masters and many paths.

People discuss seeing a tunnel of light and floating up towards a central light. What was your near-death experience?

I didn't see anything resembling a tunnel. Tucson uniformly faded out as the people around my body moved around and talked. As earth transformed into a soft fog, the other world came into view.

The first light I saw came from everything: the beings radiated light; the plants brimmed with light; the water sparkling from the waterfall emitted light. This view differed from the Divinity, that conscious center of pulsing waves over my head. The Divine emanated more of a vibrational light down to everything the eye could see. All the trees, the plants, the water, even the table and all the chairs—all emitted light from within.

So you didn't float when you saw the Source? And did you get any messages?

I didn't experience a rapid movement towards the Source, and it was more of vibrational energy than a single, powerful light. As I looked up, I knew I could float and blend into the Divine. However, I did not receive any individual message or communication. I felt endless love, and I knew that the Divine remembered me to the minutest quark. This particular knowledge of me, Lesley Lupo, (or whatever my name is Upstairs and no, I don't know what it is) streamed down from the Source that created these patterns in the sky. I felt that this light formed the center of all creation or whatever we think of as God. The Divine looked formless. I can understand how mystics call God the Source or the Unmanifest because words utterly fail in a description. The heart connection, the wonderment of the pure selfless bubble bath of love, always remains with me even with my limited human receptors.

I felt adored, which was not a concept I would have expected. Don't forget one thing: I was an agnostic when this happened. I had no time or interest in any spiritual path. Afterward, it seemed fruitless to speak of spirit, much less one that brought out such ill will from the majority of the people I told.

It seems to me that on earth we look at life as if we are climbing a ladder and the Divine is above us and therefore superior. I never felt any level of competition or a struggle Upstairs, not even a belief that there was a difference between superiors and inferiors. Older and younger souls are equal in value even though they differ in evolution. There is oneness in love. There is no pecking order, such as in one version of love is better than another.

What do you mean when you said: "… much less one that brought out such ill-will from the majority of the people I told."

Other than the two nurses who took care of me in the hospital, no one wanted me to talk about it, and the threats of hospitalization kept me quiet. Injured as I was, the spunky part of me that had never backed away from a debate was absent. I only found a Kubler-Ross book, unfortunately not Raymond Moody. I searched for spiritual study groups. One newly formed group met at a yoga studio, and the notice had the tagline *what brought you back to a sacred life?* As we shared why we had come back to an inner quest, I mentioned that the NDE had shocked me out of the agnostic/atheist stance I had at the time. People had many questions, and then we moved on to the next person. The facilitator met me at the door and asked if she could speak to me. She proceeded to chastise me for flaunting what had evidently been a hallucination. If I wanted to wallow in fantasy, well and good. However, her group was for healing. Then she asked me to stay away from the subsequent meetings.

I kept hitting dead ends. Then my friend Dana directed me to the Tucson chapter of IANDS and everything started to fall into place. I think I joined in 2010, but I never really started to attend and be involved until 2012.

Did this light stay on during your entire visit, or was there any place that it disappeared, like in the cave? Or, is there any night Upstairs?

It stayed daylight on my entire visit, and I saw no night or dark shadows. I don't think I stayed long enough to experience whether night occurred or if anyone sleeps. Earth has a yin/yang quality of the dark and the light: all I encountered Upstairs was light, timeless, constant light.

Was this ball, this Divine consciousness, the only source of light or did everyone have a something similar above them?

It wasn't a source of light; it generated all the energy waves including the ones that *produced* the light that illuminated everything. Everywhere I walked, even when I stood on the cliff and watched the light beings on the beach, we all shared that same source.

Can you describe the symbols on the backs of the chairs?

They resembled a letter or symbol written in another language that I do not recognize. In my memories, I can see but two. The closest design

I have seen here would be something like a cross between a Reiki symbol and individual letters in the Thai alphabet.

Why couldn't you read the text in the Akashic records?

Some energy veil separated me from some areas of Upstairs until I made my decision. I assume that included languages, too.

Why did you decide to return to earth at that particular time?

Good question. There was no pressure on me. It just happened as if to say, "Now you have the information, can you decide?" I felt that if I had said, "I don't know yet," they would have said, "Okay, walk around a little more." In retrospect, I began to feel tired as Meena and I went into the second building. I wonder if she waited outside the Hall of Records because the window for my physical body to reanimate began to close.

What did you do to become a mission soul?

I'm not entirely sure what you mean by a mission soul as if I had one and many others did not. I think every soul that incarnates has a mission, well, actually more than one. Usually, we have several tasks to take care of, either one at a time or simultaneously. I never got the impression that I did something extraordinary. The first incarnation in this current life was when an angel came to our group and asked for a group of us to incarnate and help with the blindfolded Bodhisattvas (Houdini Kids) that were already establishing small reservoirs of light in the shade. Because our soul group had been involved in placing them, I imagine that is why we were asked. It would be natural for the team to go down together.

Was the term Akashic records mentioned at all?

No, we never talked about any other name for the Hall. I knew it as the Hall of Records. All the drawers had something to discover and to learn. I remember the group laughing because I had a whole bunch of questions, so it seems that I am as curious Upstairs as I am down here. The reason I mention Akashic records now comes from a description I read. It also sounds like the quantum vacuum discussed by Ervin Laszlo Ph. D. in his book *The Akashic Field: An Integral Theory of Everything.* He posits that there is an information-rich field of consciousness that holds everything from the Big Bang to the distant future. The quantum vacuum links us to all the people who have ever lived and helps explain life after death. It points to a universe where all is one, and everyone is connected.

Did you have full access to your past and future records when you were Upstairs working on the placement of soul?

Of my lives? I had no clue. Other than showing me what I had done before I incarnated, we did not discuss any of my past incarnations. I focused on the task at hand, which was my decision to stay or to return.

I wonder why one would look at one's past and future? I think that the only time one might be interested in that information would be relating to the next incarnation. Many light beings work together for that process. Everything is so present Upstairs. On the other hand, I wasn't entirely committed to returning, so that kind of information might be something that we would have explored if I had chosen to stay.

When you went to the Hall, were you looking to gain information to help with the placement of the volunteers? Can you expand on the placing of light beings, older souls, into younger souls' families?

To place these particular groups of light beings, we read their energy patterns, which resemble fractals. We channeled the information to make decisions; we did not need to research. It was a combined decision, along with angelic beings.

To summarize, before the change in the mid-1800s, an evolved light being, a Bodhisattva, arrived in a family that would recognize, support, and nurture the child who aspired to a spiritual calling. They practiced their faith, whether it was a medicine path, or a convent or monastery, or a synagogue.

After global consciousness became more established, specific blindfolded Bodhisattvas (Houdini Kids) came forth to go to the areas of "shade." They incarnated into areas devoid of lightworkers. Their memories were erased without any awareness of who they were, and the families that had been chosen did not notice or support their gifts. Some were beaten and abused. Others were taught teachings that excluded others from salvation. Intuitively they knew that everyone has the potential to attain God's love. Without understanding the details, they experienced their relationship to the selfless love pouring down every second. As they found their inner spiritual light, they helped elevated consciousness throughout the whole planet and solidified the space for the third group of Bodhisattvas: Indigo kids.

When I went to the Hall, it was also to hang out and explore new ideas or watch how consciousness expanded. I am conjecturing here, but I am sure you are correct in assuming the Hall has a place in education and research.

Why is everything so light in the spirit world? Is it dark when you close your eyes?

Everything generates light. If you sat in your yard at noon and closed your eyes, you could tell that it was still light outside. I did take a nap up there, of sorts, I think. In the cave, the softer light came from the table, the chairs, and even the walls. Jesus glimmered, almost sparkly. He was exceptionally bright, but when I closed my eyes, there was no darkness.

Upstairs has a vibrational level unlike anything in this dimension. If you look at the full spectrum of light (and sound) available throughout the cosmos, you will notice that we see (and hear) a tiny little slice of all light and sound waves available. A light being might be sitting right next to you right now but on a different wavelength than you or I can experience.

Even though I did not feel as heavy as I do here, I could not see through anyone or anything. I never felt as if I could walk through a wall.

The Divine creates all the different levels, or maybe wavelengths, of light and slows them down to everything physical. It is intensely concentrated energy, not dense like a gravitational force. Everything here on earth reflects light waves. Everything Upstairs produces higher waves of energy so I, as a light being, created light too. However, every living thing here also generates a magnetic field. You are doing it right now; you're a micro-mini star on two legs.

Explain how there were no shadows under anything.

I am not sure I can. If everything Upstairs gives off a radiant glow, then there will not be any shadows because there are many sources of light, which overlap and erase any shadows. I have tried several times to draw it, but it always winds up looking like a cartoon - which it was not. I did not see any shadows under the trees nor from the buildings nor in the Hall of Records: everything generated light.

How much control does each soul have over their experience of the spirit world? Can they create what they see entirely?

I have heard theories that what we see when we first arrive reflects our deepest beliefs and desires. This idea may be right. I watched as I set up arrival settings for returning souls. Nonetheless, if we did indeed have one hundred percent control over setting up a personal picture of Heaven, I'd have landed in Willy Wonka's chocolate factory and spent my time swimming in the chocolate river. By the way, I never found the food court Upstairs shown in the movie *Defending Your Life!* I would have filled my plate with molten chocolate cake and stayed put.

When I sat with Meena and Ra-u and talked about my return in the departure room, they said that whenever I went back Upstairs, my core group almost always returned to the realm of oak forests and rivers. When Ra-u took me over to the cliff and showed me the beach and the ocean, he mentioned that a couple of times we had gone back there to swim in the water but mainly stayed in the present realm. Now, others may go into light, or sound. Some may be conscious particles flowing throughout infinity, who can say? There isn't just one pathway. Thank goodness!

Now, Ra-u also said many different dimensions exist, so I think that everyone can choose a significant amount of the environment as they progress. On earth, we subconsciously gravitate toward things that we sense on an inner level: scenes that remind us of our spiritual home.

Did you get the feeling that the light beings at the table agreed to appear in your spirit world rather than theirs to communicate?

There was no theirs and mine: everything I saw was our shared world. All the light beings at the table live in the same spirit world I do. I was home and sat with my core soul group that I work with; we have evolved together. Moreover, we all return to this world; I mean the world Upstairs with the forests and the waterfalls because they love it for themselves too. Other times we would go as a group to other realms. For example, when I returned to the beach, the entire team went and tried it. No one light being in a core group decides by himself or herself.

When souls go Upstairs, and they have a life review, do the guides help them bring back memories of their life on earth?

I think every person will have a different experience. Everyone experiences an individualized homecoming, which depends on what they chose as their life lessons and how they left their bodies. I can only speak from my experience, but, in my group, it is normal for someone who has newly returned not to remember everything about their history, either Upstairs or on earth. Life reviews help.

Nobody seemed surprised by any of my questions or concerns. Perhaps I would have gone through a life review if I stayed, but since I was "on hold," it never came up.

Did you see anyone carrying a purse, wearing glasses, or pursuing any other earth type failings like smoking a cigarette?

No, not at all. Everyone looked healthy; everyone had an average body type: no one seemed overly skinny or overweight. Kind of like a bunch of average body types walking around.

No one wore skin-tight clothing; nor did anybody walk around naked. I did not see anyone in tank tops and shorts. Everyone wore long flowing robes or loose shirts over skirts or trousers in all colors. Women wore pants, too. In addition, I saw no vehicles of any kind.

In addition, some wore simple styles while others wore ornately decorated outfits in beautifully harmonious color palettes—all except Ra-u's.

What do you mean "except Ra-u's?"

Whenever I would meditate and remember my experience, his choice of an extremely ultra-violet shirt and brassy burnt-orange pants—two particular shades that clashed—surprised me. He decided what to wear and could choose whatever color palette he wanted in the entire universe, so why pick those two mismatched colors? It never made sense to me. I used to think it takes all kinds of flowers to create a garden, including Ra-u with his messy hair and clashing colors.

Then the Ayurvedic astrologer Johndennis Govert gave me some interesting tidbits about Ra-u when he did my death/rebirth chart. In Ayurvedic astrology, Ra-u, the north node of the moon, has a vibrational color that is ultra-violet. His spiritual stone is a hessonite garnet, which is a burnt-orange, colored stone.

In my soul group, we tended to wear blues, lavenders, and purples, with one red and one more like a dark blue spruce color.

Did you see any refreshments or living spaces?

I got the impression, from when we talked, that beings would retire to places where they lived, but I never saw any. I only saw drinks when I visited in a dream right before I started work at Canyon Ranch. We had what looked and tasted like tea in lovely teacups.

Do older souls ever want to hang around with younger ones or is it like earth where age groups don't mingle too often?

Superiority does not exist regarding what level anyone has attained. I did not witness any hierarchy among the light beings that work together. Younger and older souls see each other in places for relaxation, at the large group prayer meetings, or occasionally when multiple levels of soul progressions work together on a specific project—mostly the Houdini Kids. Within a workgroup, however, the majority of light beings have progressed to the same level, like a bunch of peers. It isn't a one-room schoolroom with different levels milling about the same room. That, Meena had explained to me, was on earth.

Think of a choir singing. Many different age groups can produce an incredible range of mellifluous sounds because they blend the entire vocal range. Now think of a football team. If they are all around the same level of talent and experience, they have a much better chance of winning than taking the field with an assorted team of all the ages from pre-K to Ph.D.

Younger souls receive support and direction from their guide's suggestions, but no one overrides them and commands anyone to do anything. Think of Upstairs as a place where there is no negativity, only love; where there are no bosses, and everyone *wants* to work because it is joyous. Light beings delight in the learning process Upstairs as much as we savor our leisure time down here. They have a balance of learning and processing, but the biggest joy is an expansion that comes from discovery, assimilation, and shifting our actions based on new information. Everyone and everything Upstairs grows.

Older souls guide life reviews with the younger ones—like a teacher with a student—and more often than not, the soul lobbies to improve.

Moreover, they choose to incarnate in extremely abusive families. The being does so with the knowledge of the full range of potential futures. Before embodying, they sit with their guides to review different coping strategies.

There is another difference between a younger and an older soul when it is time to incarnate. An older soul will surrender everything for the highest good of all and sometimes go in as a sacrificial lamb to facilitate change. Younger souls primarily focus on their individual soul's growth through their choices. They accept guidance from particular light beings and angels that help.

If they fail, they will consider what the lesson was and then try again, because beings don't evolve unless they "pass the test." As far as I saw, everyone wants to advance. Evolving is the core desire: to grow and improve and become even more loving, more radiant, more peaceful.

What do you mean by the one-room schoolroom?

On earth, we have many different levels of soul maturity around us. Every group of people you encounter sorts itself out like a one-room schoolroom. Some people will be selfless and highly evolved; others that are just starting will exhibit selfish actions.

If you go to a school that has prekindergarten or kindergarten, you will witness young children as they learn to behave and accomplish projects. They learn to work with others. You will also see temper tantrums over sharing a toy until they learn to control the outbursts, no mean feat for some.

Anyone incarnating for the first time struggles with that overwhelming "fight or flight" animal part of the brain. They always live in fear and react in a self-centered way. I think one of the mistakes we make is assuming that a person who has accomplished a lot of fame or material success, and is a pillar of the society, is an evolved being who is going to be a good leader because they will look out for everyone in a protective way. Sometimes they do, but sometimes they don't.

Robert K. Greenleaf spelled it out quite plainly in his book *Servant Leadership*: A servant first, someone whose core motivation is to help others, will be a selfless leader: a leader first, someone whose core motivation is to control everything including others, will be a selfish leader. For example, you could meet a Fortune 500 CEO who has the emotional maturity of a four-year-old or you could stand in a checkout line in a grocery store and talk to an old soul who is bagging your groceries.

Emotional maturity revolves around one simple thing: taking responsibility for our actions in three simple steps. Admit the mistake, apologize and fix it, then learn from it, so you don't repeat the same error. Soul growth is based on our emotional maturity. With maturity, selfishness grows into selflessness.

When you left your body and went Upstairs, was there still a soul connected to the body in the horse corral?

No. In my situation, the body had no soul connection. I could have chosen to stay. The NDErs who have no choice but to go back still have a secure connection to the body, even though it is technically dead on Earth.

You planted older souls in places where they must discover their light within, all by themselves. Can you explain a little more about what you call Houdini Kids? And how do they relate to Indigo Kids?

Houdini Kids are specific Bodhisattvas, enlightened souls, who volunteered to incarnate into young, unevolved families, without any direction, guidance, or even any conscious memory of their connection to their inner Divinity. Initially I called them the *blindfolded Bodhisattvas* but didn't like the tongue twister. One day in a meditation, I had a visual reminder of Houdini being tied up, put into a bag, and thrown into the ocean. The words "Houdini Kids" floated above so I adopted that as the moniker.

Anyway, their ultimate goal is to find their spiritual pathway all by themselves in spite of what they have been taught. They don't complain or live in a melodramatic way, nursing their wounds. They came to forgive and while doing so, struggled to find people like themselves. They realize that even though they can fit in most cliques, they cannot stay for they came to include people, not divide into groups that exclude others.

Houdini Kids also have trouble in their high school through post-college years. There are no cliques or groups of people with whom they can feel a lifelong kinship. They can be friendly to many people from all lifestyles, but, to stay in one clique, they must put on a uniform and relinquish a part of themselves including their ability to fit into a multitude of groups. They would have to shun others. Cliques represent divisive superiority. It is impossible for them to stay in this element. They don't know who they are and must try on a lot of lifestyles before they settle into the inner journey that will reveal their true nature to them.

Ultimately, they cannot stay in one group. Some go wildly off the rails as they continue seeking, and wind up in gangs, extreme groups, or work with radical religious paths to the exclusion of others, but most bounce back because they cannot run with divisive, competitive factions for their entire lives. They live to question, and it is hard to turn that off. Many become muddled with alcohol or drugs to avoid that sense of loneliness, of not belonging. Eventually, to heal, they need to fall in love with themselves too at which point, when fully downloaded, their lives take off in an excellent direction.

Placed significantly apart from each other, it takes many years for them to discover and download their Bodhisattva level of consciousness. Most begin to transform in their mid to late forties, usually finishing up in their fifties at which point they start to meet all the other Houdini Kids around. Finally, they find their tribe.

It is also hard, if not impossible, for Houdini Kids to harbor resentment and grudges, or to be pulled into others' vendettas. They dig for the Divine light within, all by themselves, efficiently channeling new modalities in spiritual pathways. They begin to realize that in spite of all they went through, forgiveness and trying again with the same situation are two separate things. They start to look outside the box for their transcendent path while still honoring all others.

Houdini Kids came down to anchor unconditional love and inclusive, large-scale forgiveness, and to embrace differences. If we want humanity to stop the inexplicable fighting over individual interpretations of God, their philosophy of life, feuds over past wrongs, gender issues—all the things that divide people into isolated groups—then forgiveness, empathy and cooperation on a global level is a necessity.

This breaks the chain of mimicking how they had been treated. This is one of the most important gifts that they bring. The ability to see a behavior or teaching and know that it doesn't fit, that it is not something that they want to pass on to their jobs/families/friends. They are mindful, even at a young age, of how they impact others.

To accomplish this goal, Houdini Kids heal the planet by absorbing and transmuting all negativity they encounter. By forgiving their trespassers, they clear the human race of rage and retaliation that haunts our history. They heal and resist for the most part subconsciously, or I should say unconsciously. It's not that they analyze then reject the teachings or actions. However, for them to ground forgiveness, they must be placed into families, communities, and cultures that are prejudiced, divisive, and fear-based. Most of them went into families that ranged from aloof and cold judgments, or a lovely family that clung to a divisive philosophy, or they would, more often than not, drop into an abusive family and become the focus for the entire family's ill-treatment and cruelty.

It is a gut instinct, a reflex which makes Houdini Kids balk at mimicking what they feel is wrong. As children, they may be called weak or wimps for their inability to act out in a cruel, mindless way towards others.

Now some children cringe in front of a bully because they are too scared, but they rage inside and eventually act out on something weaker than them. That is not a Houdini Kid. They can be stunned by an assault, be it verbal, emotional, or physical. Nevertheless, they don't retaliate. They personalize the attack as if they were the person doing wrong. In essence, they inhale the negativity and treat the abuser as if it is justified.

Most of them have distinct memories of being taught certain beliefs or witnessing a behavior that didn't make sense, yet, when they objected, they were punished for thinking outside the box.

To help others, Houdini Kids absorb all the negativity they encounter, somewhat like a vacuum cleaner. Eventually, it affects them. Remember the vision I had? I landed in the water and soaked it up. By doing so, I transmuted the swamp into solid ground. As Houdini Kids finally do heal and begin to take care of their different emotional wiring, they morph into a leaf blower that clears negative energy around them by transmuting it, blowing it away rather than drawing it in. That happens when they value their self-worth.

When they begin to understand and accept themselves, they will rediscover their inner connection to the Divine. As they do, they clean up the muck they landed in, which solidifies the land around them.

Many people, whom I have met since I started talking about Houdini Kids, shared with me that they felt like an outsider within their family, a changeling. Many think, *what happened, did I take a left instead of a right? Where was I supposed to land?* The feeling of being an outsider hits hard. They feel alone to the bone.

Another aspect of the Houdini Kid's persona is an aversion to fighting, looking at life as, *If I must choose between being the abuser or the victim, I will be the victim.* To come down and anchor compassion and mercy, they must experience many things to forgive: i.e., early on, they are the hockey pucks of the world until they awaken. It is impossible to forgive if they have lived in an ideal setting, loved and patiently nurtured.

Another thing to add to the checklist for Houdini Kids would be feeling disconnected from many of their surroundings as a child. Whether it is philosophically, physically, or just the knowledge that any mistreatment is wrong, there is a precocious child inside, a child that already knows right from wrong and resists when being taught things that are restrictive or abusive. They have a visceral reaction to watching or participating in abuse. They know what is wrong. It is hard for them to exclude anyone because they have a high level of unconditional love for all living things.

In addition, they find themselves taking on the problems of the people around them, i.e., absorbing everyone's negativity. They are what I call *unintentional enablers. Professional enablers* actively look to surround themselves with helpless people. They have the savior complex and need to be needed so they will passively prevent the people they are helping to achieve their goals. Promises of help never materialize though they are actively advising every step their friends take and the day that they're not needed is the day they will be alone.

An *unintentional enabler* has no intention to keep people emotionally dependent; they innocently think that every time they help, the person will get it and finally stand on their own two feet. If they run into a martyr complex individual, it takes them a long time to realize the other does not intend to let go of their melodramas.

Self-forgiveness is the last hurdle. A valuable experience for Houdini Kids is to learn to include themselves in their decisions. This goal does not mean to become selfish and self-serving, but to stop being selfless to a fault. Self-love and self-confidence are two qualities that are critical for Houdini Kids to learn. Both are solidly grounded in humility. They will never be vain, or arrogant; that is the realm of the younger souls. Self-love is not such things. They have firmly rooted in humility and gratitude already. They have to add the self-love component to their journey and, as I said, learn to include their highest good in their decisions:

Is this _____ *(decision, request, person, relationship, food, purchase) in my highest good, too?*

This statement is a great question to ask yourself when making decisions. Our highest good isn't just spiritual; it includes your physical, emotional, intellectual, and financial good too.

This new sense of worth helps them to learn two important things: learning to receive as graciously as they give. (Many treat life as *I cannot sit down to eat until everyone is fed ... in the world.* A true Bodhisattva!) And, secondly (the best for last) they have to learn how to play, to let their curiosity out to explore and enjoy their beloved planet.

This new level of Bodhisattvas facilitates the arrival of another level of Bodhisattvas, called the Indigo Kids. That group can hit the ground running and accelerate change that is more widespread. Keep in mind that these Indigo children are not saviors. They are innovators. Houdini Kids paved the way for the Indigos. Indeed, many are born into awakened Houdini families, but, even so—family or not—Indigo kids know who they are and accomplish amazing things all by themselves.

Are Indigo children the same as Houdini Kids? Do they avoid any negativity? And have Houdini Kids finished incarnating now?

Indigo children are the children that I was shown in 1990 when I had that original vision of landing in the swamp, and, as we healed, we created a rock solid ground for the children to land on and run. I do not know if it is about avoiding negativity as much as it doesn't derail them.

Right now we have three levels of Bodhisattvas being born: old souls who are self-aware and incarnating into supportive cultures and families to help them with their goal to teach humanity; Houdini Kids who are still landing in the muck; and for the last thirty to forty years, a whole bunch of Indigo Kids.

Is there another group after the Indigo children?

Good question! I have no idea. I cannot imagine the Divine being limited in any way, so your guess is as good as mine.

Are there cleared areas on the planet?

There doesn't seem to be a set place: awareness moves with the population. Individuals who embody a higher consciousness congregate in certain parts of the world. While land has a specific energy, human knowledge does not originate from the earth—land reflects, resonates, and transfers it. Clarity and mindfulness arise in living, sentient beings. Think of all the different communities in the history of Homo Sapiens. Throughout history, great teachers and caring communities keep popping up all over the planet in different places. Then they shift and pop up in other locations. With Houdini Kids and the spreading of consciousness over the entire world, these places will be more cohesive and extend further. Instead of popping up and diminishing, only to pop up someplace else, knowledge will pop up and leave a fire of truth and light to burn perpetually.

Who decided to change the world and have higher souls hit the ground running?

I don't think that someone said, "It's time." Rather, as the Houdini Kids spread out and developed an individual connection to their heart, irrespective of whatever teachings they learned, the "collective unconscious" of Jung grew and developed a more productive pattern. As more and more people became aware of these inner connections to all humans, people became more heart-centered and practiced random acts of kindness and forgiveness. Consciousness continued to shift towards selfless cooperative individualism instead of the selfish, competitive tribalism.

Humanity used to act as if there was only one way to the top of the mountain and IT IS MINE. Woe to those who prefer a different path to God. Tribal thinking says: *this is the path I was taught and it is the correct and only pathway.* Why this need for such extreme exclusivity? Because of "The ONE." Many believe there is only one pathway in life, there is one way to handle a situation, or that there is only one way to relate to God. If people believe that there is just one way, and you are different, one of us must be wrong, and it cannot be me, so it has to be you.

This change of consciousness happened in the mid-to-late 1800s when light beings started to disperse throughout the whole population. Right now, billions of people are kind, polite, patient, or sharing across the world. I see it more as a natural extension of that shift, which occurred when Houdini Kids began to spread out the light instead of keeping it clustered in sacred places. In seclusion, the Divine light would have little interaction with the world. Earth was ripe and ready.

What makes us so different from other life forms? Do animals have incarnations and evolve, too?

Human beings are one of the oddest animals on the planet. We are the only animal that radically changes what our parents teach us and in every generation. Scientists can guesstimate evolution in an archae-ologically dig because of the tools they find. We know when and how metals were discovered. Let me give you an example: a grizzly bear takes her cub down to teach him how to fish for salmon. The only way he learns is by watching and mimicking his mother's actions. He prac-tices until he gets it right: his whole survival depends on it.

So let's say I'm living in caveman days and I take my son down to the river to show him how to catch a salmon. I splash around in the water, trying to grab as many as I can but losing many. He watches me, but instead of mimicking me, he notices a dead branch and says, "Mom, how about if we use this to stick them?"

We learn by trial and error, rarely paying attention to the warnings from the previous generation. Because of that trial and error learning style, we have evolved more rapidly than any other animal on the planet. In other words, we are wired *to make mistakes*. Trial and error. Error is critical to development. Yet we waste a lot of time beating ourselves up for making mistakes. We think trial and error is only acceptable in a science lab. Yet it is a fantastic tool that can be used in every aspect of the human psyche. The core of my workshop revolves around this awareness. We are going to make mistakes until we die. If I critique myself, not criticize myself, which includes judgment, I will learn from my mistakes, and learning is good for the brain. I think that if any other species made the number of errors that we make, they would be extinct.

With our inventive mind, we get to develop deeper and more pro-found levels of consciousness; a more profound range of emotional and philosophical ideas that, as far as we know, animals do not experience.

Regarding the incarnation of animals, I have no clue. My logical mind says, how can an animal evolve? If you have a worm or a robin, how would we know if they have developed? On the other hand, am I being impatient and their evolution is over a millennium? Therefore, I have no idea. The birds and butterflies I saw Upstairs seemed to be part of the majesty of the Divine rather than a soul that was continuing its upward spiral. Since it is something outside my realm of understanding, I will say that, since I have no way of verifying it, anything is possible.

When you work with a client, do you go to their Hall of Records for their information, or do you go to your Hall of Records?

I don't get the impression that different Halls exist for different peo-ple. I think there is only one Hall for everyone. But I do not access their

Akashic records. We have one or two guides with us during our entire life and they come back with us again and again. When someone endures a crisis, other guides come together to help. Perhaps grandparents come or another soul that has had the same experience. They all gather to give added support. When the crisis fades away, they leave, but we still maintain a connection with our core guide.

When the session begins, I ask all the guides, who have worked with them in this incarnation, for help so that I receive information to pass along and understand if there any blocks within. All the other guides stay connected. Many times a past life that still influences my clients will come up, and, by understanding what the lessons are, it helps us to disentangle whatever blocks them.

Do you have the ability to read everyone's Akashic records? Can anyone access these files?

No, I cannot read anyone's records without their permission. No one can tune into you and see your entire auric blueprint. When I work with a client who opens up to the process and wants information, it's a straightforward thing for me to do. Otherwise, their fields are impenetrable.

Reading someone's aura shows us what they signed up to do. This knowledge helps if they get stuck in one area or another. Most of the time, I see a behavior and can suggest a particular lesson that will help them. But I cannot just walk up to someone, look in their eyes, and scan their Akashic records. That only happens in scary movies. To do that would violate the concept of safety that is inherent in our Divine birthright.

The Akashic records, or, in my dictionary, the Hall of Records, and all the guidance stored within, is accessible to any seeker who sincerely wants to grow. Thank you for asking that question. It brings up a vital point: that it is the lack of a person's ego that allows them to access the Hall of Records. The answers about right and wrong are *within* every single individual, not far away in a library. We all have a deep craving for consistent spiritual happiness. We seek a balanced way of living so that we can unhook ourselves from the rollercoaster of "happy and sad." Not only to return to serenity and peace of mind but also to live a life grounded in truth rather than fear and denial.

With your love of forests and water, what are you doing in Tucson with deserts and cactus?

That is a funny question. Tucson has a fascinating amount of different eco-systems within a few miles. It is not all sand and cactus. Technically, we live in a high desert, but I live in a forest, a bosque, with thirty-foot tall mesquite trees surrounding me, and my home sits on the bank of a river. I also have a pond with a waterfall on my property. There are very few forests in Tucson, but the one I live in is a substantial forest. Talk about synchronicity! There are no coincidences about how I came to live in my house.

If beings communicate telepathically, are you allowed to keep secrets in the spirit world or can everyone read your mind and know everything about you?

Interesting question. I'm not sure how to answer that one. We all can communicate telepathically. That doesn't mean that it's like WIFI and we can read each other's minds. I'm not sure if anyone would be interested in keeping a secret Upstairs. Why would we? When I remember everything Upstairs, when I close my eyes and become part of it again, the amount of selfless love and support still overwhelms me. I cannot imagine the need to hide anything Upstairs, so I don't know how to answer this question.

How do the light beings help to set the curriculum, or lessons, that the soul is going to work on when they are born? What effects will their missions have on their growth?

We set our "core curriculum" by going over the "baggage" we bring back. The more we grow on Earth, the less baggage we carry back. When we fail or go backward, our energy field becomes shattered, and the brittle pieces cling to us. Moreover, with the rigidity comes heaviness. Young souls don't have much stiffness. Their lessons are small ones. Brittleness comes with an older one that fails their assignment.

Others come back shattered because of the heaviness they embody if they internalize the pain of others surrounding them. It does nothing to alleviate the problems, and yet somehow some souls think they can vacuum up all the pain on Earth. It causes them to shut down, which does not benefit anyone; neither their immortal soul's growth nor the ability to help, not even the individual suffering soul. If people attach great importance to the outcome of their advice, believing that this is what the other must do, on an intuitive level, the recipient turns away because they can sense the attachment and do not integrate the lesson.

Once we review whatever lessons we chose, we then go back to Earth to practice. Let's use an analogy. Let's say that when you return Upstairs, you bring back something that people would define as the baggage of unresolved lessons. Are they really unresolved? Sometimes we fail miserably. The human fear factor takes control and sends us into a negative spiral. However, sometimes an unfortunate life experience—that appears to be a setback—is there for the soul's growth. Some choose to feel the grief they caused others by returning and being the recipient of similar anguish.

However, this information is not a carte blanche permission to ignore anyone's pain and say, "Oh, that is their karma." We are obliged to help those less fortunate, and that is part of our choice; so, to step over someone and ignore them is to fail at one of our lessons. However, it is the emotional attachment that we humans have to our own advice, our pushing our opinions on others, which sometimes shuts down people's acceptance of said ideas.

I'll use an example of a past life regression that I did with a client to illustrate this type of soul balance. I have a client, Mary P., who had been a talented ballerina. She had been born in Paris to a working class, broken family. Before she turned eighteen, she attained enough fame to be the star of a dance company that toured Europe and America. While on tour, she met a wealthy man, Bruce K., from an old European royal family.

They had a passionate love affair, and, although he often hinted at a future with her, he would not commit. Then she became pregnant. Finally, Bruce unveiled his plans. He had been courting another European woman from a prominent blueblood family. His wedding day wound up being the same day that she gave birth to their daughter.

Mary was devastated. Bruce's family, including his new wife, formally adopted the child. Mary was allowed to participate in her life, but only with the governess present, never alone. She could not let go of the betrayal. So here in my office, fifty-three years later, Mary cried and said every time Bruce was in the paper (or his wife or his other children) a new lance of pain and resentment impaled her. She never even dated again.

I didn't know this backstory when I began her regression. All she asked was if she ever had a past life with a man named Bruce. She told me only his first name.

I tuned into Mary's energy field and channeled that in the late 1700s, back in France, she had been a man called Mark, and Bruce was a young woman named Betty. Even though Mark (Mary's) family was prominent in shipping, he had three older brothers, so Mark bought a commission in the army to make himself a name. He was an officer in the military that bivouacked on a large country estate where Betty (Bruce) worked as a milkmaid.

During this time, Mark had an affair with Betty who subsequently got pregnant. When Mark heard this, he panicked and volunteered his group for battle sooner. At the same time, he lied to the girl about being called up and avoided all contact except to make several fake promises to come back.

A healthy son was born, but, after a decade of waiting, Betty died alone and heartbroken. The family servants kept the boy on, though Mark never saw his son or acknowledged him. He acted as if the incident never happened. He eventually married, drank, sailed on ships, had many lovers, and died at sea.

From the immortal soul's perspective, the soldier and the dairymaid have both lived different sides of a valuable lesson. In that life, Mark (Mary) was the abuser and Betty (Bruce) was the victim. Now in this current life, the roles have reversed. Mary and Bruce have experienced both sides of the same lesson.

In the past life, the soldier needed to learn how to be selfless. First, Mary had to determine the lesson by playing the role of being selfish Mark. What does it feel like to hurt someone? Bruce played the role of Betty and had to learn to hold one's self-worth a little higher and not pine for fantasy. Many times if someone hurts someone else profoundly, they will volunteer to come back to experience the pain that they caused.

When they both left their bodies and went Upstairs, they took with them all the mistakes that they made in that lifetime and would gently heal the errors Upstairs. Light beings, who are their guides, sit in to help them face the sorrow they caused. With the level of love and light all around them, they eventually process what they need to learn. Then they work with another group to plan what lessons would benefit their soul's growth upon its return to Earth.

Picture an energy pattern around you that resembles a multicolor kaleidoscope. As you learn and grow, it becomes more fluid. If you make mistakes and regress, it becomes more brittle. In addition, the varying degrees of fluidity and brittleness eventually will influence your new lesson plan.

When a new soul arrives back home from Earth, the re-orientation process is gentle. After that, they have a life review, and their mistakes will set up the next round of lessons. So, in that earlier life with the soldier and the dairymaid, they would have sat down, objectively and compassionately reviewed what they had done, how they felt, how the other felt before they signed up to go back and change places.

In this lifetime here and now, Mary—who was the soldier and the narcissist the first life, the person who abandoned the young girl after seduction—is the victim. And now Betty, the dairy-maid who experienced abandonment and died of a broken heart, encounters how a selfish lothario lives. At least Bruce has progressed to acknowledge his child, even if it is in a different family structure.

After this lifetime, they will both return and work out the new lesson plan for their next class. For example, if Mary lets go of her jealousy toward Bruce's family and social life, she could move on and not be connected to Bruce or the lesson again. Even if he never experiences complete remorse for the way he used her and must come back to repeat the experience, another soul would come down that would need to learn the lesson of abandonment. However, if they both accomplish their mission at the same time, they will come down for a happy spousal relationship to solidify the growth.

Do the older souls have to coerce the younger ones to take on different or more challenging life lessons?

There is no pressure, no pushing a specific agenda or goal upon anyone. All the challenges or courses are up to the individual to choose. Souls want to grow, want to learn, and want to try again, even if they work many lifetimes to learn one particular lesson. They keep at it without any aura twisting.

About seventy percent of our soul's growth takes place Upstairs. Younger ones might have upwards of eighty percent growth taking place in the "schools" up there. I am using quotation marks because the schools Upstairs are nothing like the ones down here. There is no pressure. It is hard to explain how much joy goes along with expansion, learning, and growth. That's the ultimate goal, growth.

Do souls return to the same core group with each incarnation? Do they ever switch? How are soul groups set up Upstairs?

When I was Upstairs and had left the cave, I traveled over to the town which was my home. I saw what looked like several other villages at varying distances from my own. Meena explained that these communities house younger souls and as they grow, they move along into another town. To understand I used the allegory of schooling and thought of first-borns as being in baby playgroups. As they progress, it is like Pre-K, Kindergarten, etc. all the way up to Post-Grad studies.

Advancing souls tend to come down in groups and go back to the same area and team. Missions, both for personal growth and helping somewhere else, are agreed upon before the souls incarnate, and then they are evaluated upon the soul's return. Sometimes many life lessons are crammed into one lifetime. Other times, souls can take one lesson and break it into several lifetimes. If they fail the contract altogether, they go back to a less challenging level. Some evolve faster and may change groups. I'm guessing here, but there may be souls who progress faster and change core groups as we would if we skipped a grade or two.

It is a bit different from the Houdini Kids. They are the blindfolded Bodhisattvas, volunteers who choose to bring light into the darkest parts of Earth consciousness. They are born into the youngest families who are light beings that just started to incarnate. Therefore, they will endure a lot of abuse and neglect or misinformation.

They volunteered to be the trailblazer in a particular area. In addition, in doing so, they generated a brand new vibration that is a completely new way to connect with the Divine. They break down the tribal, more primitive consciousness, which is something that stops most individuals from feeling an innate connection to all humans.

When they find the Divine light of their immortal soul, the blocked energy is released into (and lifts up) what Carl Jung referred to as the collective unconscious, something that throughout history has been shaped by society. Now, because we are becoming global, earthlings if you will, this connection transcends individual communities and connects us to all human beings on the planet. Science today, primarily physics, is validating Jung's theories by finding through our magnetic energy fields that we are all already one. We don't understand it yet. Think about it: when we clear and grow stronger in our life, we drag all the others along with us. Life grows upwards.

In addition, when they die they go back up to the "college" section of Upstairs and the younger souls of that birth family go back to the "kindergarten" section. It is unlikely that their paths would ever cross again.

Does a soul have the ability to say "no" to a particular lesson or job? And how much do they know about the families that they pick, even the younger souls that are evolving?

Again, an individual saying "no" just doesn't compute with my experience Upstairs. No light being is coerced. Some beings learn at a faster pace; some beings choose to take more time to grow. Both pathways lead to perfection. If someone wants to take their time, and everyone else intends to finish a particular lesson, they may join another group.

It's a little tricky for us to conceive of this here on earth, but all life, at every level, yearns to grow. After a certain amount of time Upstairs there is a restlessness that increases within individuals to come back to earth (or wherever else they go) and test what they have learned so far. Don't forget that most of the work and schooling we do is Upstairs. Earth is where we come to examine what we have learned to expand ourselves. Work Upstairs is as valuable, and desirable, as leisure time is down here.

What constitutes a younger soul? Is it based on the number of incarnations?

I think the label "younger" would relate to their soul's evolution, not how many incarnations they have experienced. Many choose to take three or four lifetimes to learn one lesson. That is accepted and supported. Others will combine three or four levels of learning into one incarnation that is a lot tougher, but that choice is also recognized and encouraged. As a result, some older souls may have fewer manifestations than some youngsters. Soul growth comes from passing the tests that we choose. It manifests through rising above being controlled by fear and living a more selfless life and caring about the welfare of others.

When are they no longer considered a younger soul?

As the Divine grows and new souls emerge, they tend to cluster with the other new ones nearest them. In the group, they will develop at different paces, and the best analogy I have already referenced: the structure of a school, from baby playgroups to Ph.Ds. Younger souls focus on controlling and dissipating primal violence or rage. After that, they focus on not placing themselves in harm's way. Then they are given leeway in what they learn so I would guess that might be when one would say they are no longer younger souls.

Some children have different aptitudes for learning and even skip grades; others take longer and have to repeat. Different teachers teach in different areas. Yet the prayer circles that have everyone in them will have all levels present. As the soul evolves, it's drawn towards an area of service they like. On earth, we lean toward careers that interest us, and we take the appropriate curriculum in school. If I study to become an anthropologist, I will take particular classes that are different if I major in Renaissance literature or accounting.

However, there is no better or worse Upstairs. It isn't as if one area of service gets you more brownie points than the other; it's what the individual chooses. Our soul's evolution doesn't mean we will all become homogenized into carbon copies of each other. Our soul's growth occurs when we accept entirely all the dissimilarities as equal to our own, and we love *increasing* the variations of differences as we evolve.

Is there any grief or sorrow in the spirit world?

I did not see it anywhere except in that healing room, but it was contained within each soul that was there and nowhere else in the chamber. An overwhelming amount of love, compassion, and joy permeates every bit of consciousness there. When I felt sorrow, it dissipated almost immediately. I also knew that the group saw it. They knew why, even though, at the moment, I did not. Such levels of love and acceptance inundated me. It would have been impossible to maintain any negative emotion. No one mentioned or dwelled on it at the time because they knew that it would heal. Sadness could not stick to me because so much love, light, happiness, and joy circled me.

Is it universally true Upstairs that all souls wish to learn and evolve, or do some souls not like to learn and grow and would rather play in either the beautiful waterfalls or playing with the animals in the ocean?

I hesitate to speak "universally" for anyone else. There are many different realms, but all I can talk about is the field I experienced. In that realm, we do play, too. We relax in the beautiful waterfalls, or beaches, mountains, hills or cities. My group was taking a break and swimming at the waterfall when asked to volunteer.

I cannot imagine anyone up there refusing to learn and grow. Immortal souls want to add to the overall consciousness and at their own pace. Spiritual evolution brings absolute joy, an experience many have as their goal.

Do you know what happened to Hitler after he committed suicide?

Oh! Such a question! I have no idea what happened to Hitler per se after he killed himself. Because he is not one of my favorite people, I would hate to think that after what he did, he is up there in a cloud of light, healing. However, that's my *human* reaction and not my immortal soul's response. I would imagine that it is just as I said for others: souls that became evil probably stay in the specialized healing place for quite a while (whatever that is Upstairs) before they come out and face their life review.

By the way, suicide is not a natural progression for souls. A person committing suicide is in the bleakest and most despairing of emotions. They feel extremely isolated. In addition, most of the time, the core lesson is learning to ask for help. It is difficult for me to generalize in this area because there are too many motivations that wind up with the same outcome. However, many people who commit suicide are good at giving love and helping others, yet cannot ask for help themselves. Hence the lesson. They have painted themselves into a corner and cannot see a way out. In the midst of that despair, their energy field collapses from within. Hope stretches our energy field away from us out into the world where it finds a way, just as a tiny trickle of water finds the way for the coursing flow behind it. People painted in the corner feel no hope.

When the soul returns, there is neither judgment nor punishment. They are tenderly placed in a separate place and restored to strength. Then they go back to relearn the lessons that they did not fully integrate the first time, augmented with more lessons about stretching their field of energy out when despair comes into their lives, and they begin to cave in. It's rather like taking a sabbatical during college. Eventually, they must return and finish the lessons. Afterward, they are always surrounded by love and support. Eventually, they have to come back and undergo the same circumstances, i.e., the family, the culture, or the particular health issues that caused them to give up. Suicide is never handled as a simple shortcut to a comfortable place. It is always regarded as a mistake.

Outcomes considered "successful" Upstairs could be different from how we perceive that word down here. I think one of our mistakes is that we automatically assume that a person who has become a successful political leader, or has risen to the top of the business or entertainment world, is somehow going to be more mature and wise and know more than anyone else. Sometimes that is the case; however, sometimes it is not.

Conversely, I have never agreed with the saying, "Power corrupts: absolute power corrupts absolutely." One can see the real character of someone after they have been successful. Younger souls base their core identity on their surroundings, on their riches and power they exert over subordinate people; older souls base theirs on their character and service to others. Younger souls become conceited; older souls become confident. Don't forget, self-confidence is rooted in humility.

Do souls that act in an evil or harmful way on earth know that they are going to do this when they come down?

No. Souls do know that it is a highly tricky test. Other times, they incarnate into the ultimate of degradations a human can endure, or with faulty wiring in the human brain. In other words, people who take those particular tests are evolved souls and utterly aware of the possibility that they can elevate their consciousness in a tremendous way or risk failing and falling back, which erases whatever growth they have accomplished so far.

For example, let's revisit Hitler. When we try to comprehend how someone could orchestrate such a shocking turn of events, experts use his terrible childhood as an explanation to understand what formed him. I would put his childhood side-by-side with the youth of Mahatma Gandhi or Nelson Mandela, against the abuse and appalling experiences they endured. They pushed through the hatred they experienced, forgave where they needed to forgive, and went on to become stellar humans in ways that continue to amaze and motivate us.

Hitler had a choice and failed miserably. He had some extreme childhood experiences, but ultimately he flunked and went backward. He will go back to learn why he crumbled. Small individual crimes are not what I mean. Those are usually younger souls who are struggling to control their aggressive impulses. A collapsed old soul is evident when someone has the social impact of a Hitler or Pol Pot, someone who triggered mass suffering. The fact that they can intensely affect vast numbers of people adversely is what I mean by "collapsed."

While light beings are Upstairs, teachers strengthen their inner structure so that when they return and incarnate, and experience the expected challenges, they can rise above the pain to inspire others with the lessons that we have learned.

In summary, Hitler was an older soul who chose a big challenge and failed wretchedly. He saw the trials that he would have to undergo, and he went anyway, which caused a domino effect that still causes agony today.

How does the soul's growth affect their karma? In other words, is there a significant difference between a younger soul who makes a mistake and an older soul who makes a mistake?

When a younger soul makes a mistake, a dense spot attaches to their energy field and, as long as it takes (including lifetimes if necessary) for them to fix it, the mass will stick to them. It drops off when they learn the lesson and pass the test. It looks like a blip in someone's aura: a spot that lacks an energy flow.

When an older, evolved soul makes a mistake, they sense the dullness, and they usually don't like the feeling. They often take steps to correct it right away. In that case, they don't have any karma fasten on to them. If not, a brittle energy spot irritates until they fix it.

Picture a marathon open to all runners. At the starting line, jostling competitors could cause beginners to fall flat on their faces, even hurt themselves to the point of leaving the race. An older, experienced runner may miss a step, but he would quickly correct it and get right back in step with the other runners.

Everyone makes mistakes, even the oldest, purest, most selfless beings. An older soul has no problem in apologizing for his mistake. Younger souls will rage against the universe, the family, their sports team, their boss, or anyone and everyone. It's never their fault. So, as we mature and can honestly admit a mistake and learn from it, we are much less likely to repeat it.

Do family feuds continue in the spirit world or is it something learned in childhood?

I saw no evidence of any harmful emotions Upstairs or competition of different levels of growth. That seems to exist solely in the human realm, and, yes, it is learned as a child. Hate has to be taught; it is not natural whereas love is very natural. Anger bubbles up but passes away unless one has been trained to hate. When I was born in Chicago, my particular group's mission was to anchor a higher level of forgiveness into the collective unconscious that would help to stop the feuds that have run for centuries. No baby is born despising anything, much less another person. We are born with our animal brain fearing others not in our tribe, but, with all the cultures traveling all over the world, we have the unique chance to raise our children to love their faith, country, and culture while enjoying the differences in others rather than being threatened by said differences.

We all have to let go of past pains. You cannot drive forward if you stare in the rearview mirror. Releasing past hurts is a big job for us humans, but is the foundation of true forgiveness. Then we must conquer a much more challenging form of absolution: we must learn to forgive ourselves for the mistakes that we make.

Are there only certain people who have the job of assisting this shift of consciousness, or are there some ways that anyone and everyone can help?

I didn't see individual light beings assigned to the job to create the shift, and others ignore it. It is the purpose of all the lessons combined into one, to help, to love and cherish each other on earth. Unconditionally.

We *all*—and I mean every single sentient being on earth,—can *immediately* affect the shift and growth of good old-fashioned peace on earth, goodwill towards men. Yes, even your pets help this energy, too. Everyone can help, must help, for the most significant change to occur. The more that people work on themselves to find that spark of the Divine within, the more we can clear away the primal fight/flight programming, which makes us fearful of anything that is not known to our tribe.

In addition, the more we practice the "Random Acts of Kindness" philosophy, the quicker we can change the energy from competitive to cooperative. In my workshops, I raise the challenge for people to practice random acts when they drive their cars. For example, begin to let people into your lane and don't feel ruffled if they fail to say thank you. Practice those random acts selflessly. The more we do it, the easier it becomes. In my humble opinion, it is one of the most significant ways to effect a change. Some people say that they cannot make a difference. Yes, you absolutely can. Start with the random acts. Step by step.

Vote, sign online or paper petitions, find and use sites like *Ecosia. org*, a search engine that plants trees (at no cost to you) whenever you use them to surf the web (twenty million and soaring), the *HungerSite.greatergood.com*, a place you only have to click for others to commit to donating food. Five hundred million cups of staple food so far have been distributed. And look to support people who are working for a positive change like the *Nas Daily minutes* (https://www.facebook.com/nasdaily/) on Facebook (over five million followers in fewer than two years) or *The Optimist Daily*, a newsletter that shows all the excellent business people around the world who are helping to create a permanent change for the better. Connect with like-minded people.

Many ancient souls with high levels of awareness are adding specific vibrations to the planet, yet they aren't speaking to multitudes like the Dalai Lama or Deepak Chopra. You could be talking to an actual sage when you are buying popcorn at the movies. It has nothing to do with what they do as a job: it has more to do with their goodness, their humility, and their consistency.

Are there times when many souls come together for a special meeting Upstairs?

Many souls get together to meditate and send light and selfless love on a regular basis. When someone suffers a crisis, their guides convey light, hope, and ideas to help them get through that time. Other evolved souls join in, especially if they endured the same problem when on earth. These extra helpers move away after the person heals.

People who sincerely ask for help to solve a problem receive the information because they are open and absorb it. Individuals who do not ask for help are still surrounded by light and love. Yet they are shut down, so they cannot receive much. Learning to receive (which makes us vulnerable, no easy task) helps us to fix this problem.

Enraged people have such a force blustering through them and outward that it drives away any and all help. All their guides can do is to watch with selfless love in case the negative energy field collapses. It is not an issue of the soul's safety. Light beings cannot suffer pain in any way by that force. The originator of the rage is the only one hurt, along with those who, unfortunately, choose to live with them. They become blocked by the flow of negative energy that hate and rage generate.

When did you get a tarot deck?

I received my first deck in college and then again in the fall of 1988 when I was thirty-six. I bought a copy of that tarot deck and studied the pictures again. I hadn't had a pack since the age of twenty-four. I meditated on the images and kept a journal about my impressions. I remembered how Bonnie had taught me and would pull a card for the day asking for inner guidance or would ask what this card means to me now. I intended to be aware of my intuition and reconnect with my spiritual side that I had left behind in 1973.

Did you know if the mission that you initially volunteered for was a higher-level task than the placement of older souls?

My original incarnation was a mission to help shift consciousness and to generate forgiveness. I cannot call it higher. I can call it different. Placing older souls in families and communities helped to elevate the light within and to raise the light on earth. It adds to the collective unconscious and creates a vibration to inspire hope in younger souls.

Particular Bodhisattvas were asked to volunteer for the Houdini Kids' mission. Think of my group—about a third stayed behind. We who left did not think less of them as though we were better or more heroic. When older and younger souls work together, there is never a feeling of higher or lower. Would you feel superior to a five-year-old because you know long division and they do not? I think not.

So overall, do children pick their parents?

I wouldn't say that children pick their parents; instead, I would say that the immortal soul and the family choose what they all need to learn. A younger soul receives a lot of guidance to help with the possibilities, almost the same as saying they know the requirements that they have to experience to evolve. Therefore, when anyone begins to set up an incarnation, it is always with the understanding of what's on the curriculum and the separate challenges they will encounter. In addition, don't forget good karma. You also choose according to the talents and skills that you have already learned. You don't forget them and always start out again at ground zero. Every lesson, every *aha* moment, every epiphany and loving thing you have right now in your life comes with you to the next. Unless you are a Houdini Kid. Then the assignment is to put the knowledge so deep within that it takes decades to remember and bring those to the surface.

What determines which lessons the youngest incarnating souls are given to study? Is there a general plan even though we have our progression?

During their earliest incarnations, souls have to become accustomed to their human construct, which means they react in a primeval manner to all the negative emotions hard-wired into the human brain and struggle to overcome their baser animal instincts. Overcome, but not eradicate. Also, the illusion of separation from the Divine is disorientating.

Older souls meditate and connect to their immortality within, their spark of divinity, and therefore don't have the same pressures. They will have different demands based on their curriculums. All souls crave growth, and there never is an end to how we can refine and improve ourselves. Look at the trees that live for 5,000 years. They still grow every year. It may be only a tiny ring or a few leaves or needles, but they do produce. Growth is everything.

Every soul begins the same way: learning to control aggression. They will try many different kinds of belligerence, experience different lifetimes of playing the villain, always struggling to build a conscience and integrity—even between lifetimes—and face the evil within. Eventually, they succeed in developing impulse control, and they balance what they've done. And, they learn to forgive others rather than extracting a payback.

Then they will try many different victims' roles. Many times people allow painful situations to continue because they are afraid of setting boundaries. They couldn't, or wouldn't, take that leap of faith and stand up for themselves. Whether they are the victim of prejudice, of a crime, or of an abusive family, they will struggle and learn to rise above powerlessness. However, not by putting on armor and carrying many weapons—that puts them back in the aggressor cycle.

They overcome that helplessness by learning to forgive themselves and release dysfunctional relationships. They develop self-worth and learn to receive. They create a style of living where they attract their peer groups; loving, kind, and forgiving people who are already happy.

It's not a timing issue. Having five lives of incarnating as an aggressor doesn't mean that a soul has to experience five lives as a victim. It's only for as long as it takes to have an aha! moment, which permanently transforms them.

Let's say that someone who is evolving dies suddenly. The level of spiritual awareness that they have accomplished will be, more often than not, the same level they will re-incarnate in their next lifetime.

Once a being has dropped the cycle of being the aggressor or the victim, they have choices to take their growth and education to a higher level of possibilities. Then their lesson plan branches out into many different areas. Souls always want to better themselves.

At that point, they have the choice of what they develop and what areas they are interested in Upstairs. At that time, they will begin to mentor the younger ones. Younger souls have less of a choice of what classes that they will take, rather like the schooling on earth that, in the beginning, is a structured curriculum. All souls need to learn the basics. As the souls evolve, they choose the direction for their growth.

When a being returns Upstairs, distinct helper souls, who are more developed than the younger ones, review the "test results" and guide the choice of sessions Upstairs in preparation for the next incarnation. As souls evolve, they gravitate towards different areas of service. Many go to the areas where they learned their hardest lessons. In addition, we all have down time where we will explore diverse interests, and, at other occasions, just play.

How do older souls cope with mundane details since they seem to see a bigger picture? Is there something that prevents them from just sitting down and doing nothing?

Mundane? I'm not sure if there is anything ordinary Upstairs, but I only had a glimpse. Think again of trees that have lived 5,000 years. Can you imagine a sequoia that is 3,350 years old thinking *What a beautiful view? The wind in my branches, I am pretty tall. Maybe I'll stop here.* Again, all consciousness desires to grow, to enhance itself. There is no end to growth! Ever! The universe is expanding.

The more a soul incarnates and helps, the more selfless they become—but there is no such thing as perfection. I think that, with the concept of infinity, there cannot be "perfection." Perfection means I am done. *Finito.* There will never be a soul that can't grow. I imagine boredom would prevent them from just sitting down and doing nothing.

Bhagavan Sri Ramana Maharshi died from cancer, yet his life essence, his soul, could separate from the physical experience of the pain. His disciples cried and pressed him to try surgery again, even though the former ones had failed. There are many pictures of him smiling, holding up his rotten arm as he replied, "Why are you so attached to this body? Let it go!"

These higher light beings can show us that you can get to a level of awareness where it doesn't hurt to be a human. (Or watch your sports teams lose. I'm still working on that one!)

I have a beautiful anonymous quote about peace that I found on the Internet: *"Peace. It does not mean to be in a place where there is no noise, trouble, or hard work. It means to be in the midst of those things and be calm in your heart."* This is one of my favorite sayings that I read almost daily.

Pain (and the fear-based behavior it triggers in our DNA) protects our physical body, so we notice traffic, cliffs, or rattlesnakes. Nevertheless, it isn't supposed to be a motivational force, and thus, with experience and the development and progress it creates, younger souls evolve into older light beings. Everything Upstairs is timeless, so I'm tempted to put quotation marks around the words older or younger. Let's say more or less patterned by their configurations in their auric blueprint? Just kidding!

How soon before death does a soul leave the body?

Now that's a fascinating question. I can only speak about what I witnessed; I'm sure that there are other different experiences. Many years ago, before hospices, I used to work in an extended care nursing home. If the family couldn't, or wouldn't, turn up when the patient was dying, I snuck into their rooms and held their hand. I saw many people cross-over. Then I had my own near-death experience. In addition, my father died in my arms. In every instance, the soul left the body a few seconds to several minutes before their death. All natural feelings stayed centered in the body as the soul witnessed their demise.

That is different from when the soul prepares to go home. The disconnecting process could be compared to leaving a summer cottage to go back home. In the last few weeks, you stop buying large quantities of food and eat out more. Little things get packed away so that you won't have a mad packing frenzy the last day. The soul starts a disconnect process for two to three months before it leaves.

When souls return to the spirit world after incarnations, do they view the spirit world as a new beginning or something else?

In my experience, it is a continuation of where they lived Upstairs before they went down to their last incarnation. When you return

Upstairs, you have full memory of everything you signed up to do. It's like an actor playing a role. When he goes back home, he is no longer the character he played.

We go down to earth to incarnate and play our roles. When we die, and our immortal soul returns Upstairs, does the last character have a separate consciousness that returns to another plane with all our other incarnations?

Okay, you are asking if, when I incarnate and go back Upstairs, the role I played, Lesley Lupo, independently goes back to another area of the spirit world? Therefore, there would be two Lesleys up there, and all of the incarnations I've ever lived would reside somewhere up there, too? Is that what you mean? Yes? Okay, interesting.

When I was doing life reviews with the younger souls, we would use the line of their history—all their incarnations and different lesson plans and contracts—to help show them where they had succeeded and where they might have to redo the lesson again or practice a little bit more in a particular area. They could recite all their past lives like an actor remembering all the different roles that they have played. Therefore, in my realm, that concept of various fields for each incarnation would probably not happen. How would souls evolve if their lessons were not integrated into their souls?

However, I could never say, "That's not possible!" There are many different realms available Upstairs. Even though what you ask seems contrary to what I experienced, I could not say an unequivocal "no" to that. It might be something that exists in many different realms, perhaps your own?

Who are mediums communicating with, using that analogy of movies and roles—the soul or the character?

Good question. Let's say I have a client who wants to connect with a loved one such as a grandmother. If the grandmother comes through, I will be speaking to the grandmother's immortal soul. However, the eternal soul will also have a memory of the role that was played as the grandmother and will come in as a female even if Upstairs that soul prefers to have a male form. The love that exists between these two immortal souls transcends any role or barrier.

Did you know you could rewrite your contract when you first volunteered or does the assignment represent a commitment to a lesson or mission that cannot change?

I don't remember a lot of details about when I volunteered. I described some of it in the previous text of the book, but I don't remember any "escape clauses" when I came down to be born in Chicago. When I returned, Meena shared that because I love the earth so much, I overrode or changed, the time I would go back. At the time, it sounded as if it were an impulse. In addition, older souls can break their contracts. So, apparently, I had the power to stay or change my contract and my impression is that not everyone can. Younger souls have much more rigid arrangements, as would an older soul who has yet to complete their mission.

Why didn't your experience in the spirit world help you to balance your life quickly when you returned?

First, we must let go of the belief that anyone who has a near-death experience (NDE) or a spiritually transformative experience (STE) automatically floats back to earth and walks on water. With the abundance of literature now published, we are capable of integrating these lessons much faster. When I had my experience, it was 1988. Unfortunately, I did not find Raymond Moody's work and had to struggle all by myself to make sense out of what had happened to me. Meena and Ra-u had told me that it would be tough until I integrated the experience. When I was Upstairs, and they spoke of "struggling for a few years," it was entirely different from a few years on earth time. Yet, now that I have integrated it, it seems like minutes have passed since I realized the problems of attaching too much to a role and how that could detach me from my immortal soul's consciousness.

The accident and the NDE happened many years ago. The welcome I encountered when I woke up in the hospital was a constant threat of being institutionalized and heavily sedated. Don't forget, I was an agnostic bordering on atheism when this happened. I did not have an established spiritual life, nor did I have any spiritual support group or community that would help me to integrate what I had experienced. Whenever I tried to share what I knew, or the joy that it inspired within me, the reactions ranged from a loving *there, there dear, it was all a silly dream* to ridicule to anger with full-blown verbal abuse. On the other hand, some people would put me on a pedestal of perfection gifted with some magical power that was equally as uncomfortable.

The reactions caused me to go into a survival pattern of denial: put my memories of Upstairs, and all it entailed, on the back burner and get back to day-to-day life. Yet I promised myself that *someday* I would go back and revisit those memories. However the detachment kept me sad and disconnected. Any traumatic experience can isolate you from those who mean to help but are helpless to understand.

Every night, as I went to sleep, I would crack open that door and remember bits and pieces from my experience. As my mind quieted and I blissfully drifted off, I could feel the same level of selfless love. However, when I opened my eyes in the morning and had to deal with the day-to-day scramble that I lived in, it seemed as if the spiritual side of me went off somewhere else.

My primary goal had to be stabilizing my health and home life, yet the Divine doesn't like to be put on the back burner. Little by little, spiritual people, books, and workshops kept crossing my path.

The taste of selfless love always simmered deep within me like it simmers within every single human being. The more I meditated and worked on myself, the more my immortal soul came to the surface. Once I settled into my new home and established a spiritual path, I reviewed what happened and put the pieces together. That is when my soul group Upstairs taught me a few lessons on how to merge the human consciousness with my immortal soul. Nothing like teamwork!

Don't forget there is no sense of time Upstairs. We can look at timelines with regret, but that is collapsing energy rather than expanding it. Why judge it? The point is that I learned. I integrated the Divine and human parts of me. Now I can center myself, forgive myself, and fix mistakes when they occur, rather than struggle to be flawless. Perfection is not my personal goal as it means I have nothing more to learn and I believe, or I hope, that that is impossible. I want to learn and grow, perpetually, in this lifetime and at the place between lives.

After you returned, when did you have a clear and consistent access to the spirit world?

I have a hard time with timeline questions. Let me think. When I lived at the ranch, I went into town, bought a tarot deck, and started working with the archetypal imagery and journaling in a three-ring binder. That was in the fall of '88. At the same time, I began meeting people who led spiritual lives. Before, when I had these extraordinary visions, I couldn't tell anybody. Now I could communicate with Dana and LuAnn. That opened the door.

In '89, I went to England and the door opened further. I would have to say that the connection returned there, in England.

After I left the Tanque Verde Ranch in '91, I went to meditation retreats here in the States and ashrams around the world, particularly India. I learned to still my mind. That is when I had constant access to the spirit world in a matter of minutes, seconds sometimes. Previously, I struggled to feel the connections that are always there. You know, it's not as if we have to call the angels and our spirit guides from another place in the Universe. They, and the connections to feel and communicate with them, are always present, like your telephone. All it takes is a clear and consistent focus on the union, the link to our Divinity within, to be able to access it.

Why don't all people who return from an NDE remember their near-death experiences?

I don't know. Meena and Ra-u asked if I wanted to remember my experience or not. In my case, they advised me to recollect even though it would make my life more difficult. Perhaps there are other souls they encourage *not* to retain the experience, so they don't have such a difficult transition when they return.

The fact that no one believed me and even threatened me with a psychiatric hospital scared me into being quiet—for years. For that reason, I wonder how many people remember the encounter but still are afraid to talk about it.

In one lecture that I did at the University of Arizona with Dr. Gary Schwartz, he wondered if the number of NDE recollections correlates to the number of people who easily remember their dreams. In spite of the fact we know that everyone dreams, few consistently remember them, and almost all will forget ninety to ninety-five percent of their dreams unless they make a concerted effort to journal them. I'd love to see a questionnaire that asks the NDErs how many frequently remember their dreams as I do.

How can you be sure your NDE happened and was not a hallucination?

Think of the awareness you have right now as we talk. You can feel everything around you, like the couch you are sitting on, the shoes on your feet, the glasses on the bridge of your nose. All the rest of your senses map out your world—from showing you the room all around you to hearing the outside world or Janice, perhaps, as she does something in another place. Tomorrow, could anyone convince you that you hallucinated your memory of our talk today? No. There are facts burned into your mind, substantiated by the gazillions of brain development that can recall this conversation which we are having. You will not remember the total minutia of sensory facts, but you know it wasn't a dream that we talked.

That is the same reaction I have to my experience Upstairs. Hallucinations are like dreams: they evaporate when we are out of them. I remember the experience as vividly as I remember our talks and they don't fade away.

I love to research things, and that thought had often crossed my mind, especially in the beginning when everyone close to me insisted otherwise. Fortunately, there are more and more qualified accredited scientists researching NDEs. One is Dr. Bruce Greyson, Professor of Psychiatric Medicine and Carlson Professor Emeritus of Psychiatry & Neurobehavioral Sciences at the University of Virginia.

His study compared near-death experiences and psychotic hallucinations spanning over thirty-five years. In the context of his research, he found significant differences between NDEs and psychotic delusions.

NDEs happened during life-threatening or other extreme situations, unlike psychotic experiences. NDEs were rare and didn't repeat. They occurred in people who weren't diagnosed as having a mental disorder, weren't intoxicated, nor had been diagnosed with a metabolic disease. All of the above were consistently present in hallucinations.

The content of NDEs differs from a delusion. An NDE is accurate and detailed. The substance is patterned, structured, and in a non-random organization. They are consistent across thousands of individuals in different cultures. Many times, they include verifiable perceptions such as out-of-body perceptions of the surroundings, even in other rooms. They are unrelated to events in the physical environment and compatible with religious or spiritual traditions.

Experiencers recall their NDEs as real or hyper-real. The memory of the experience persists over time and remains vivid. It also retains the original details. None of that is present in psychotic hallucinations, which are usually forgotten in minutes. In addition, hallucinations almost never stimulate a spiritually transformed life.

On December 15, 2001, the highly respected international medical journal *The Lancet* published a thirteen year study of NDEs that Dr.

Pim van Lommel conducted in twenty different Dutch hospitals. This paper is one of the few NDE studies carried out prospectively, meaning that Dr. van Lommel developed a questionnaire and gave it to a large group of people who, during cardiac surgery, experienced the cessation of their heart and breathing function.

Using the results from the interviews, the doctors discovered which patients had experienced NDEs. This type of study gives scientists a group of non-NDE patients to compare with those who had NDEs. That, in turn, offers scientists much more reliable data about the possible causes and consequences of the near-death experience.

For example, in the past, some researchers have asserted that the NDE must be merely an oxygen-starved brain conjuring up a hallucination, called anoxia, after the heart has stopped beating. This study casts doubt on that theory, and, in the words of its chief investigator, cardiologist Pim van Lommel, MD, "Our results show that medical factors cannot account for the occurrence of NDE."

Dr. van Lommel and colleagues list ten elements of the typical NDE:

1. Awareness of being dead.
2. Positive emotions.
3. Out of body experience.
4. Moving through a tunnel.
5. Communication with light.
6. Observation of colors.
7. Observation of a celestial landscape.
8. Meeting with deceased persons.
9. Life review.
10. The presence of an impassible border.

Some people who have NDEs wind up with one foot on earth and one foot in the spirit world. Is this the same for you?

Absolutely. Even before I came back, Meena told me that's how I would exist here, a bridge for consciousness. I would hazard a guess that all NDErs live like this. Moreover, I would think that all Houdini Kids who find their connection to the Divine wind up existing in both worlds. However, it is not a room only for NDErs. Anybody who has had an epiphany, a spiritually transformative experience, will be living like a bridge.

Spiritual insights are not a level of awareness that is open to only a few select people. Anyone can attain it. Through faith and patience, they can crack through the illusions of separation and integrate the Divine into their everyday life.

In addition, what about our play? Sometimes I think that people believe the spirit is too somber and doesn't accept the playful side. I think we have to blend them.

To sum up, exercises that still the mind, like quiet, contemplative prayer and meditation, journaling, help everyone to exist in both worlds at the same time. In truth, everyone has the potential to build that very same connection, or relationship, to their inner Divinity. I'm aware of my contact with the Divine inside me, that's the only difference.

Did your near-death experience automatically convert the rest of your life on earth to helping others?

I helped people before my NDE. I studied psychology and gerontology and worked in a nursing home. It's a connection to my inner divinity that has changed so that today I can't imagine living any other way. I think the shake-up that occurred was more in my spiritual practices. I had put any and all interest in sacred experiences on hold. However, just before my NDE, I found myself listless and disconnected.

That being said, countless numbers of people do great works of selfless service without having had anything remotely close to an NDE. One of my friends is a complete atheist and one of the most ethical, moral people I have ever met.

I will continue to help as much as I can. I want to write more, do my workshops, make more jewelry, but also play and travel and visit friends and family. That's part of it. However, a mission soul is not someone who works, works, works, and does nothing else. Even Upstairs we take time off, goof around, and play. Therefore, playtime and relaxation are both parts of my life down here. As far as learning how to watch my sports teams from a place of non-attachment goes, I'm still working on that one!

Is a near-death experience a wake-up for people to get back on track for their original mission?

I honestly don't know. I think every NDE experience is unique and each could serve a different purpose. Don't forget: for most humans, it is the choice of the immortal souls when they leave.

I am not sure I could comment on anyone else's individual mission. We all have a series of tasks that overlap. I rarely ever see a client with only one purpose for being here.

It's not as if the guides Upstairs use an NDE to reel you in to check on your progress or give you a pep talk. They can do that when you are dreaming or meditating or through other happenstance in life. The point of free will is to take the odd happenstance and use it to empower our growth—at least in my realm. Again, I hesitate to speak for all; there is no "one path," no "all" when we talk of spirituality.

If you had to boil the entire experience down to bullet points, what did this NDE teach you?

Bullet points? That is so hard! This was a deeply personal, individualized experience. What I had to learn, many people might already know; many may not. However, I'll give it a try. For me, I would have to say that one of the most important revelations is the power of a regular practice of gratitude: i.e., a gratitude journal. I've been aware of Ra-u's last words, *remember, every breath is precious,* and applied it to every day. It's also interesting to see the recent data on how gratitude journals can rewire the brain.

Remembering that the world is a one-room schoolroom and, by extension, every group, family, congregation, fan base, organization, board, is a one-room schoolroom and, unlike Upstairs, this causes conflict. Treat others without judgment or superiority. This doesn't mean we can't be discerning, but that is different from condemning all differences as wrong. Be patient and objectively observe how they treat others, especially people of lesser means. That will highlight their place in the panorama of life. Accept people as they are or walk away. My favorite instruction from my workshop is this: *if you open the box and it says assembly required, put it back on the shelf.*

In addition, the one room schoolroom applies to us as individuals too. Some people have part of their psyche as adult, responsible, and successful, yet another part is very immature. One can have a success in business but not the private life, or vice versa. As we grow, try to be authentic and make sure your body, mind, spirit is in balance and growing equally.

Next, those seemingly insignificant random acts of kindness are going to unify the global consciousness into the *peace on earth* mode, which we all crave in our core. Practice those until you drop.

All you have is right here, right now. There is no yesterday or tomorrow. Be present.

We all have a deep well of eternal hope; no one can show it to you. You must keep the mind still and dive into yourself to find it.

We are giving up an idea of "The One," that primal animal mindset that there is only one pathway in life and no one else's is equal or better than mine. We see that many paths lead to the top of the mountain. And all are equal.

Cooperation will eventually move competition aside, especially in our spiritual, or inner, journeys. Individual differences should be stimulating and cherished, not scary.

PART TWO: EPILOGUE

A s I sit by my pond and await my grandchild's first birthday, I remember my initial impression of my return home, to Heaven ... *As the cowboy ran to the main ranch house, the stable all around me began to change. The barn, the horses, the people, and the fences all began to fade away into an intensely bright fog. I wanted to linger, to stay where I was and see them all: the cowboys and the guests, the horses, even the manure on which my body lay. A surge of vulnerability passed through me as I watched it fade away.*

An endless river of shimmery particles streamed past like a breeze and whooshed around me. I did not move, yet everything around me started to shift and change. Triangular patches of intense blue-white light hovered around me so that nothing bumped or jostled me. These splashes of energy appeared to be conscious, yet I could not recognize what, or who, they were. I felt the separation from the ranch increase as another world developed. I expanded again, lighter than before. A soft crackling buzzed around me, reminding me of the whooshing sounds that I had heard when I saw the Aurora Borealis in Canada.

As my world in Tucson gradually grew dimmer, another realm slowly emerged. Faint outlines of a thickly wooded forest, impenetrable and still, slowly took form. Large oak trees with thick branches stood fully leafed out with ferns clustered at their trunks. Bright green velvety moss partially covered the trunks and roots. Small-multicolored star-shaped flowers carpeted the forest floor. Their unfamiliar scent wafted over, pungent and intoxicating. As this new world came more into view, selfless love covered me and filled me with the purest and most intense sensation of indescribable joy.

Behind me, a large creek about twenty-five feet wide noisily bubbled and splashed over a bed of mottled brown rocks. Off to the left, the trees thinned, and a hollow appeared. The transition from the earth plane to this place—whatever it was—happened so seamlessly that I wondered if this realm had always surrounded my life in Tucson but on another level of energy that existed beyond the human scope of perception and comprehension.

In spite of the thickness of the forest, there were no shadows underneath the foliage. No sunbeams broke through the canopy. I could not discern any particular light source. On the contrary, each twig and leaf, each flower and rock glowed with iridescence, seeming to be lit from within. The entire forest shimmered like sunlight on water. Radiance shone from every plant, tree, rock, and flower, which revealed vivid colors that I had never seen before. A life force flowed through the greenery, and I could see it. The forest manifested itself and danced before me. It all seemed familiar somehow, a dance that I had taken part in many times before.

Quite unintentionally, one recurring thought ran through my mind: I have to remember this. I have to remember it all. I reached out to touch a bush right next to me; the wide green leaves were bright and slightly translucent. They glistened yet were dry to the touch. It resembled a hologram, however denser.

A faint rhythmic tune pulsed just beyond my hearing. I wondered if it came from somewhere in the distance. I began to move as things snapped into place around me. Moreover, in spite of the fact that my mind was still alert, I felt much groggier than I did after the accident.

As I moved around, selfless love hung around me like fabric, a veil of spun sugar, sticky and sweet. Even though it felt palpable, it permeated me like energy: I soaked it up from my head to my toes and embodied the essence that saturated all around me.

I knew I was in Heaven or what I would come to call Upstairs. I, or some part of me—at that point I had no idea how to define myself—existed beyond my body on earth. I was still mindful of me, my mind, and that I was dead. That knowledge never left me as I looked around. I felt more at peace than ever before.

I knew this was real. Never once did I feel stupefied. It was not a dream; instead, I was in a heightened sense of an authentic reality. It was so ultra-real that for the first of many times, a sentence popped into my mind: This is real: earth is the illusion.

Afterward, I returned to a severely damaged body and not only did I have to undergo a long and tedious physical healing, but I also had to recapture my spiritual path, dropped so many years before. After what I had experienced, I could no longer doubt that I did indeed have a spiritual component to my psyche. For the first time, I allowed synchronicity to happen. As my body healed, many spiritually gifted people crossed my path, people I probably wouldn't have even noticed before.

We never stop growing, at least I hope not. In writing this book, I understand on a deeper level the greater significance of my near-death experience, especially when people light up upon hearing the entire description. By answering questions with Leslie Klein, I was able to put my NDE into a chronological order and to see it as it happened, instead of a series of memories. That, in itself, deepened my understanding of the beautiful qualities of my encounter. It has connected me on a much deeper level to the remembrance of being flooded with selfless love, something that I can repeat a lot easier now. I had never taken the time to contemplate and remember the experience in its entirety until I wrote the entire unfolding of events. I just recollected it all in bits and bobs—a video in my mind of this scene or that one. Some memories made me feel more transcendent than others, and that would change too, perhaps because of the mood I was in, or depending on which one of my lessons was front and center. More remembrances came to me as I focused and wrote: subtle things that were not as riveting as the love and peace I felt, but essential details nonetheless. Case-in-point: the colors Ra-u wore or the pattern in the grasses as I walked toward the waterfall.

There have been many changes over the last twenty years, mostly for the better. Max Roser, an economist at the Institute for Economic Thinking at Oxford, created a web site on it,* he maps the history of the world over the last thousand years or so. There is now more global compassion for people. We have come so far when we view our history in its totality. Case in point: in 1800, eighty-seven percent of people lived in abject poverty. By 2000, it dropped to less than twenty percent.

There have always been those heart-centered people across the world making changes, quietly and behind the scenes. Now more individuals are beginning to collaborate. Enough Houdini Kids have spread out across the world to cause a tipping point. My nickname for this movement, this shift of awareness, is *cooperative individualism*. The herd

---

*   www.ourworldindata.org.

instinct, the biological fear-based drive that causes an animal of one pack or herd to fight to the death against their own species from another pack, is beginning to be supplanted by unconditional love and empathy for all living things, all sentient beings. In addition, we are finding delight in the different philosophies and pathways to the Divine.

One of my favorite memories happened during a visit to Puttaparthi, India. I was at a dinner party put together by a father and son, textile dealers in a nearby shop. Devout Muslims from Kashmir, the guest selection were many of the people who were staying at Sai Baba's ashram. Of the dozen or so people, we ranged from many different countries and included such diverse spiritual paths as Christian, Jewish, Buddhist, Sikh, Hindu, and Taoist. We discussed our inner questions ranging from our view of the Divine to how to attain inner peace and what mattered in life. In spite of the range of different faiths, no one fought or dismissed any other pathway. The feeling was that by sharing, we were capable of seeing a more complete picture of God. It was a beautiful dinner, and we talked until the wee hours. The outpouring of love and understanding between us was refreshing. It reminded me of the famous drawing of blind men fighting over the description of the elephant that they were touching. Instead of fighting, we shared, which intensified our own personal connection to God.

Today cooperative businesses are outstripping competitive ones. During high school in the late sixties we were bullied by the jocks for eating a little tub of yogurt. Today, doctors regularly prescribe probiotics, and organic food is one of the top trends in the food industry in America. Many countries are following Bhutan's lead and pledging to grow only organic and non-GMO foods; the latest to set this as a goal is Russia.

Life has ups and downs: all you have to do is watch the news. You will see the news organizations go out of their way to depict people doing horrific things to each other and anything that moves. The brutality, the cruelty that we see hurts every human being. Individuals who are helpers have the same shutdown I had, the sense of complete and utter helplessness, while we watch people, animals, even nature treated harshly. It can engender a total feeling of bitterness, a throwing in of the towel because we are powerless to help.

For me to continue whenever life knocks me down to one knee, I look back at the year I was born, 1952. From that point, I look at all the evidence of social and conscious growth, all the manifestations of expanded consciousness, from Jesse Jackson's original Rainbow Coalition to an international e-zine called *The Intelligent Optimist*. From the Air Pollution Control Act of 1955 (which did little to prevent air pollution but made the government aware that this problem existed on the national level) to the fact that, as noted in a recent study, eighty-one percent of Fortune 500 companies voluntarily published sustainability reports. So many other things have changed for the better that it brings hope back into my heart.

We still have a long way to go, but don't forget to look back at how far we've come if you want to keep your hope alive. We can always justify our baser impulses by referring to our "animal instincts," or reptilian brain, or the survival part of our brain. A notion is one thing; we all have them. Watch me watch my quarterback throw an inept interception. But the action we take in addressing these urges is another thing. We always have a choice. We need to assess our responses and release fear-based reactions.

I disagree with the words *It wasn't meant to be*. It seems helpless as if no matter how hard you tried, it wasn't going to succeed. Some say the words to soften a mistake, others as a fatalistic excuse. I don't believe that it is a "soul lesson" that causes me to have a setback in business, health, or love. The soul's lesson comes *after* the problem: i.e., how do I deal with it? How can I better myself by learning this lesson? We all face many seemingly random things in life, and one can choose to learn from them or not. I choose to say, "oops, I made a mistake, learn from it"—which makes me smarter—and move on, trying my best not to repeat it At least more than three times.

One of the lessons I learned that has kept me going, given me hope, is the very last message that Ra-u said to me as I started to incarnate, "Remember, every breath is precious." It has become my mantra. We take so much for granted every day, the material things we have, even the paved roads under our tires. Every morning when I wake up, I remember *every breath is precious*. I always want to be in the beauty of gratitude and appreciation for what I do have, for love all around me, for the knowledge and the wisdom that has become the cornerstone of my life. It helps me to keep my eye on my future goals.

I now do a lecture called "The Science of Near-Death Experiences" at the Canyon Ranch in Tucson, Arizona. At first, I was petrified of public speaking, afraid of the audience response. I thought that because the concept of death is so terrifying to people, they would turn away. On the contrary, it has been well received.

I think there is a reason why we are more willing to question and change our perspective on living. Baby Boomers have marched and kicked down every door rooted in fear and now are facing the final door on the road, one steeped in dread. The opinions that people generated in the sixties is still present, a belief followed by actions which demanded equality for all races and genders. It heralded the ability to choose what affects you—for example to vote at eighteen instead of twenty-one. All this started a model that still today permits us to ask anyone, no matter what his or her place in society, a simple question. "Why?" Why must we stick to beliefs that split humanity into a pecking order? Equality is becoming a concept based on oneness, not sameness.

That same curiosity, mixed in with empathy, is now challenging the idea that to age gracefully, you must become invisible, retire from community action, just go and sit out on the ice floe all by yourself. Retirement in itself is new to the human race.

Before the Industrial Revolution, the older generation was held in high esteem for the production of goods. Their experience made them instrumental to producing good quality products. With the advent of production line manufacturing, the elders were not fast enough, so in the mid 1800's retirement with a meager pension started. So did depression and alcoholism. Without a purpose, we falter. In the history of humanity, people work until they die. Many times, they switched to a job that would match their physical skills. People who connect with each other and feel helpful are the ones who live the longest, healthiest lives.

Read *Super Genes* by Deepak Chopra and Rudolph Tanzi to understand how that works. Alternatively, watch the video, *If Your Name is not in the Obits, Have Breakfast* by Carl Reiner. It explores the number of people working between the ages of ninety to a hundred. Baby Boomers now have turned their sights to the subject of death and dying and talk about it openly, which is something that had only been done behind the closed doors of hospitals and nursing homes.

While my life before my near-death experience was a fantastic life, the richness of my life today is more significant and directly relates to the lessons that I learned. Talk about being present! Living as if right here, right now, is all I have has affected how much baggage I allow myself to carry in my backpack. In addition, as I got older—and much wiser—this new information has allowed me quiet, consistent joy based on facts, not delusions.

Moreover, even though I have this incredible peace, I still have the hard-wiring of the animal brain, those reflexes that constantly, consistently pull up the fight, flight, or freeze reactions to stress. If I'm objective about that part of me—without judgment—then it is so easy to catch myself when I begin to tip over, and to right myself before I fall off the rails into fear, panic, and hopelessness.

Just start from this premise: every breath is precious. You are loved. Live the love you are in now, and be ready for more to unfold. Have faith and slow yourself down. Add patience to your daily practices. Everything will work out for you, even if sometimes it doesn't look as if it will. The Divine has your back. Stop beating yourself up. Get used to making mistakes; it's the quickest way we learn. The Universe sends us love in a reflection of how we love ourselves; so the more we love and take care of ourselves, the more we attract love from our all relationship levels. Include yourself in your decisions; it brings back a sense that you do have a lot more choice in life that you imagine, and, when you realize that, you can genuinely heal and find inner peace. Get out there, live, love, and laugh!

PART THREE: REFERENCES

APPENDIX I
Messages from Spirit, a Reading with
Evidential Medium Suzanne Giesemann

Leslie Klein was curious as I spoke with him of my NDE. His
knowledge of spiritual matters led him to ask many insightful
questions. In addition, being of a scientific mind, he remembered details and connected some dots, which I had not. He asked me
a logical question that I had never considered since my NDE in 1988.

When I was caught in the stampede and returned Upstairs, there was
a table with eleven beings seated at it; I was the twelfth. When Meena
and Ra-u discussed the day I had initially volunteered—the time we
were all swimming by the falls—ten of the group had stayed behind.
So Leslie posed a reasonable question from the description that there
were eleven light beings at the table, but one I had never considered:
which one of the eleven was Sean?

The thought that Sean was up there had never crossed my mind. I
never considered which of the light beings he was when I first sat down.

Even after my NDE, I never thought about the fact he might be part of my core group that helped to advise me.

For years as I re-experienced the appearance of the forest and the table of twelve in meditation, the only light beings I could see clearly, and therefore paid attention to, were the ones immediately on my right and left. A significant ball of energy in the middle of the table blocked me from perceiving anyone on the other side.

However, once he asked me that question, it seemed to throw me off. I could not meditate. I could not get to that level of stillness that I had done before. Yet, almost every night I would dream about a man who did not look like Sean, or at least as I knew him on earth. With the man as a guide, almost every night in my dreams I relived memories of all the unnoticed synchronicities that happened since my NDE. I kept getting the sense that there was a message from Sean that I could not quite understand. I asked Gary Schwartz to recommend someone without saying why. I wanted to work with a medium I had never met, someone who knew nothing of my life or my NDE. He mentioned Suzanne Giesemann so, in May 2015, I called Suzanne and asked if she could help.

All I told Suzanne was I couldn't connect with someone on the other side who was trying to give me a message. She did not know if it was a spiritual guide or someone who had already crossed over. As this is an exact transcription of our session, please excuse the typos.

Transcription of Suzanne Giesemann session: May 2015

Suzanne: All right, so sitting in our awareness that all is Spirit ... I just surrender my focus on the physical world and ask my team to step in now. And we set the intention to hear from any loved ones, any spirit on the other side who most needs to speak with Lesley Lupo this morning, and any guidance that will be most helpful to her. We'll do our best to just relax and fill this room with Love and gratitude for the best possible experience.

Okay, just give me a few seconds now to shift over; all right, hmm ... okay good high energy here! The very first image that I had is a big red heart like a Valentine's heart; looks handmade, red ribbons ... paper glued together. That's the first time I have ever seen it in a reading, so that is lovely. Then I am hearing, "Of course I would be here, why wouldn't I show up?" This is coming from a male. All right, he's giving you a great big hug. He says you are doing good work. I think that that is him saying that, but I'm being pulled over here to where more guides are. Let me just be quiet for a minute ... They are ... "they" being ... I believe these are your guides, but they are slipping a robe like theirs down over your shoulders. There are trees all around, and they are saying no, they are not your guides ... "You are one of us, but this you know." And they are so grateful to you for having made the sacrifice to come back into human form. "We know that it is not always easy for you, but what is easy for you is slipping back into that place where you know truth ... where you know who you are, and so you play ..."

They're showing me a balance beam. "You play this role most deftly," ... hmm ... "balancing like the angels on the head of a pin. It is very easy to fall off, but you maintain your balance far more than most. And the peace and the love that you bring to those in your field is tangible to us. These words you do not need to hear, for we transmit them to you mentally. At all times you are aware of our presence, but perhaps it is good for you to hear them externally today for a boost of confidence and simply reunion." ...hmm...

They are showing me that there are times when you say, "Why am I not with you guys now? I'd rather be over there," but you are sort of smiling ... (laughing) ... okay, all right...

Did that first part resonate with you, Lesley?

Lesley: *Yes very strongly. The first man is a man I knew here named Sean. The large red heart was the first valentine he made me out of ribbons and red construction paper.*

Suzanne: Okay, let's keep going ... I don't know if Sean would have ever had a motorcycle, but it would have suited him well because he feels like a free spirit. And I see him riding across the desert with his, oh ... well ... I don't usually see them, but if he had hair it would be flowing out behind him, but just that feeling of free spirit and going all out, but at the same time what I'm feeling is a very mellow presence ... somebody who was not too easily ruffled. He's showing me, "Oh, yeah, I could have a temper." but there's just a chilled out feeling around him. Hmmm, does that feel right?

Yes, very much so, very little rattled him. His temper—if you could call it that—came in when he was protecting others.

Yeah, yeah, yeah, okay ... and very casual dress. I want to be in blue jeans and something ... almost like a ... fringy ... oh, no wonder! This is the seventies! Like a fringy vest; like a leather vest; like a suede vest with fringes on the bottom.

That was mine ... he bought it for me in Santa Fe ...

He's tapping a watch, but it is a reminder. It's a reminder: "Don't forget" or "Be on time," or "You need this reminder because you are not punctual" ... that's uh ... he's telling it to you. He's telling it to you and kind of laughing ... hmmm ... No. He means something else ... "We have a date," he says, and he's still tapping that watch. Does this make sense to you? "We have a date." OK ... Oh ... oh ... okay: He's going to be one of the first to greet you ... not that you don't have the right to other loves in your life or haven't had any others, but you and he were like ... wow, I'm seeing like a twin flame ... That's the image that he's showing me ... so you were a couple? And that you had a pact, and he's guiding you. He's showing me that he's been guiding you. He's one of the guides from the other side ... "Don't be in a hurry. You still have work to do, and it's steady" ... "steady" meaning there is nothing more that you have to do right now because you are perfectly on track and doing what you are supposed to be doing. You are bringing light in. It is pouring in through you. I also see some artwork or jewelry.

Yes, I make crystal jewelry.

And artistry in that way. You are aligning with somebody that does artwork. I see ... hmm ... colorful paintings or mandalas ... open air market fair and people are just drawn to the light from all of that. Okay, back on track ... So it feels as if you may have been questioning your purpose here still, even though you know very intuitively why you're here ... why you are doing the work, you are doing. But your guides are assuring you there doesn't need to be any spike or ramp-up or make any changes ... you are, of course, always experiencing incremental growth, more and more peace, more and more of a settled feeling, and it's all perfect. Okay, now is a good time to ask any questions.

Well, the reason I reached out was ... when he first died ...

I just have to report: They are showing me something falling off a shelf ... some object falling on the floor of its own accord. They are just acknowledging it.

Oh, well happens every time I am in the shower. I have a wire thing that you hold your soap in the shower and in spite of a bunch of rubber bands to stop it from falling, every time I do a prayer or blessing ceremony, and as soon as I put my hands together for water to make a pool of for the blessing, the thing falls off. And only then. I am not touching it, and it only does it when I pray, and I take that as confirmation.

They are saying, "That is our way of showing you the Oneness, and that we are there with you, and all is in the right order, and you have created the correct energy field for doing your work, which is replenishing, energizing ... reconnection ...

Okay, so the thing is, he and I came down on a mission: we are part of a group up there ... this is what I was shown when I had my near death experience, that I came down with Sean, with a bunch of them; we went down to help make a change. I was born in '52, and I got involved in the peace marches and the women's marches, civil right; we were supposed to come, land, get things moving and then he and I were supposed to go back Upstairs together when I was twenty-one. And then I...they said that I loved the earth so much that I opted out and I stayed. I just want to check on something....

Let me just tell you what I am getting before you go on: They are showing me sheets of paper like parallel lives, like the possibilities that lie ahead. And I want to get this without being influenced by your question because it is very clearly being shown to me right now that there were, there are always multiple possibilities of future, of the future. You chose one, but the other was so strongly in place that there was a shuttling, but in the dream state. The soul was jumping back and forth between the two lives, trying to reconcile the two and bring them into alignment so that the physical aspect of you could integrate this shift that you had made. This soul was enacting both possibilities. It was a "shuttling" until you integrated all into this line of possibility, this reality, which now has become yours. "You made the choice to stay, but you have not allowed yourself to fully live it or your thoughts have held you back ... tying you too much to Spirit, to our side. This is why we were showing you the balance beam. You really get the whole Spirit side, but the human side has yet ... since you made the choice to come back it is up to you to fully balance the human side as well, and it is out of balance, for you have not fully accepted your return," and they kind of laugh a little ... it's a pleasant tolerance ... ahh ... So you are here for the long term. You will enjoy the grandchildren...

I just got a very unusual hit, and I'm going to bounce it off of you. It's a little aside here when you said "the group of twelve" earlier ... I am also part of a group of twelve, and they're showing me that this "twelve" and the concept of the twelve disciples is an aspect of consciousness that repeats itself in a ... hologramatic fashion throughout humanity, and that these groups all carry the same consciousness of the group of twelve disciples that we can read about in the Bible. Even though I know nothing about that, they're showing me that spiritual aspects repeat themselves and have broken themselves off from the Great Oversoul to these consciousness groups, and when you opted out to stay, that is where you shifted over to the other plane of reality, the other possibilities of which there are infinite numbers, but that one was always held in possibility, and that is why the dream state lasted so long ... you had to readjust ... wait a minute ... wait a minute ... they are showing me the word ... and ... the "trajectory," that's it: the trajectory of possibilities ... okay...

That is a word I use all the time, trajectory. I even like the word "arc" better, but for some reason when I am channeling, I use the word trajectory.

(Laughing) Oh cool! They weren't going to let me talk until I had gotten that one out! Excellent. I have never used it ever ... I mean, in reading, in this sense. Beautiful. Any other questions?

No, you answered the questions before I asked ... I've got a lot to meditate on.

Cool ... I love it!

Even with what Suzanne had channeled, I still felt like there was one more piece of the message. In spite of everything, my logical mind sensed a thread out of place. If we had popped apart and he returned, what else proved that to me? What else could validate the fact I had jumped the contract?

At Canyon Ranch we have an excellent clairvoyant named Pat Bruckman. I contacted Suzanne first because Suzanne knew nothing of my experiences and I wanted objectivity. However, with a little thread out of place I decided to ask Pat. I popped into her office one day when we both had a break. I said the same thing, "I'm having trouble getting a message from someone on the other side." That is all I said.

Pat immediately started channeling and got a very strong message from Sean. I wrote it down because I had not had the foresight of taking in my cell phone and recording it. Sean had one clear message: *Please don't worry about the fact that you left New Mexico. I could have come to Chicago with you too, and I didn't.*

APPENDIX 2
Scoring of Lesley Lupo's Reading with Suzanne Giesemann by Gary E. Schwartz, Ph.D.

INTRODUCTION

In most instances, it is impossible to verify independently the veracity of a person's near-death experience regarding their spiritual experiences. It is one thing for a person having an out-of-body experience, seeing and hearing things taking place during surgery, for example, and later verifying critical aspects of what they experienced via nurses and doctors. Lesley provided some significant independent corroborations of her out-of-body experience in the horse corral via the reports of the cowboys who witnessed and participated in what happened the moments after she sustained her injuries.

However, it is another thing to verify a person's near-death experiences when they have left the physical plane and are having profound experiences in higher realms. How do we know which, if any, of these experiences are veridical?

A compelling approach to addressing this fundamental question emerged spontaneously when Lesley felt the need to have a private reading with Suzanne Giesemann, a gifted evidential medium. You have read about this particular reading in the first appendix. Given the historic nature of this unique reading, I proposed to Lesley that she carefully rate the information using a formal scoring employed in my Laboratory for Advances in Consciousness and Health and that I would write a brief report as an Appendix summarizing the findings.

As the opening quote reminds us, Lesley was super-careful not to give Suzanne any details about herself—either her life in the physical or her experiences "Upstairs."

As you will see below, Lesley's scoring of the reading reveals surprising confirmatory evidence of significant aspects of her spiritual proficiencies in addition to her life history in the physical.

Method

I first instructed Lesley how to isolate potentially rateable items from the raw transcript. Together we determined that there were two types of articles in the transcript, which Lesley could accurately score: (1) literal physical items—i.e., items related to her life on the earth, and (2) authentic spiritual items—i.e., items which referred to specific events and experiences Upstairs. Although other types items could potentially have been scored, such as metaphorical and philosophical statements made by the medium, we decided to stick to those items which could be most justifiably rated.

It turned out that the transcript contained rateable eighteen physical items and eleven spiritual items for a total of twenty-nine items. I then instructed Lesley how to assign ratings of one to six to each of the items.

The instructions for the scoring procedure are listed below:

1 = A clear miss (i.e., the information provided by the medium is inaccurate as applied to the particular deceased person)

2 = A stretch (i.e., the information vaguely fits the deceased)

3 = Possible fit (i.e., the information could fit the deceased)

4 = Probable fit (i.e., the information could be interpreted as being a genuine fit/hit, but it is not completely clear)

5 = A clear hit (i.e., the information can easily be scored as being accurate—i.e., the fit is obvious)

6 = A super hit (i.e., the information is especially meaningful and significant, also, to be precisely correct)

Besides rating each item, I requested that Lesley provide a sentence for each item explaining why she assigned her rating. This description ensured that Lesley rate each item as thoughtfully as possible.

Table 1 (including at the end of this report) lists (1) each of items, (2) the type of item (Physical = 1, Spiritual = 2), (3) the 1 – 6 rating, and (4) the explanations per item. The items are listed in the order they appeared in the transcript. I sat with Lesley as she rated items 1 – 10 to confirm that she fully understand the procedures.

Results

The first figure plots the number of items receiving a given rating, separately for ratings 1 – 6. This plot combines the physical and spiritual items.

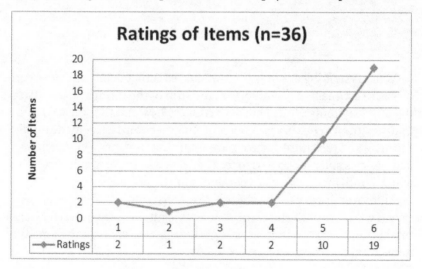

You can see that only 2 items out of 36 (i.e., 5.6%) were rated as complete misses (1's). In contrast, 10 of the items (27.8%) were rated as definite hits (5's) and 19 of the items (53.8%) were rated as super-hits—for a total accuracy of 82.1%.

If we use a slightly conservative estimate of total accuracy and include the 2 items that were rated as probable hits (5.6%), this increases the overall accuracy of the reading to 87.6%. These findings provide a statistical confirmation of Lesley's more informal personal analyses of the reading.

The next figure separates the items into Physical (n=28) and Spiritual (n=8) items and displays the data as percentages of their respective item totals.

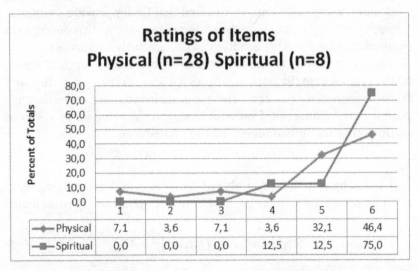

	1	2	3	4	5	6
Physical	7,1	3,6	7,1	3,6	32,1	46,4
Spiritual	0,0	0,0	0,0	12,5	12,5	75,0

What is striking about these two curves is that using the more conservative estimate of accuracy (i.e., the sum of the ratings of 5's and 6's), the physical items total accuracy score is 78.5% and the spiritual items total accuracy score is 87.5% percent. In other words, the medium (Suzanne) was even more accurate in obtaining information which verified Lesley's spiritual experiences than she was in getting information which confirmed Lesley's experiences in the physical.

Moreover, if we use the slightly less conservative estimate of accuracy (i.e., the sum of the ratings of 4's, 5's, and 6's), the physical items total accuracy score increases slightly to 81,7% whereas the spiritual items total accuracy score rises to 98%!

Discussion

The overall pattern of the findings justifies the conclusion that Suzanne Giesemann's spontaneous reading of Lesley Lupo is extraordinary and provides essential independent validation of main aspects of Lesley's spiritual experience Upstairs. This is unique in the history of near-death experience research and deserves to be celebrated.

Items, Types, Ratings, Explanations
Table 1

ITEM	T	R	EXPLANATION
Okay, good high energy here!	2	5	**A clear hit. I felt an elevated level of energy when I was Upstairs, clear and fresh energy the flowed through**
The very first image that I had was is a big heart ... like a Valentine's heart	1	6	**A super hit. For Valentine's Day, with the help of the House Mother, he flooded my dorm room with cards and heart-shaped candy boxes**
Of course I would be here, why wouldn't I show up?" This is coming from a male ... ... all right, he's giving you a great big hug	1	6	**A super hit. I had contacted Suzanne for two reasons, the first because I was trying to tune into Sean. I had just realized that he was at the original table in the forest when I went Upstairs. All I said was I was having a difficult time tuning in to a message from someone on the other side. That is all. She did not know anything of my NDE, nor, at this point, did she know who Sean was**
He says you are doing good work.	1	5	**A clear hit. Sean would acknowledge that I am doing good work.**
but I'm being pulled over here to where more guides are	2	6	**A super hit. Now she is channeling my soul Group**
Let me just be quiet for a minute ... they are ... they being ... I believe these are your guides	2	6	**A super hit especially as it pertains to my NDE. Sean was with my soul Group during the session**

ITEM	T	R	EXPLANATION
But they are slipping a robe like theirs down over your shoulders	2	6	**A super hit. My soul Group is showing her who they are to me.**
There are trees all around	2	6	**A super hit. Suzanne is describing the forest where I arrived.**
no, they are not your guides … you are one of us, but this you know	2	6	**A super hit. Now they are saying who (and what they are to me) which corrects Suzanne's explanation of their being guides**
they are so grateful to you for having made the sacrifice to come back into human form	2	6	**A super hit. This validates what Meena, Ra-u, and I talked about regarding my decision to stay Upstairs or return to earth.**
We know that it is not always easy for you…	1	6	**A super hit. This is the second reason I had contacted Suzanne in the first place. I felt disconnected and alone in my journey. I wasn't sure what I was accomplishing**
but what is easy for you is slipping back into that place where you know truth, where you know who you are, and so you play	1	5	**A clear hit. I am often in meditation reconnecting with my inner Spirit, especially as I wrote the book. I felt disconnected from earth. It is so easy to sit and "be still" when I feel alone on earth because I am not alone with my soul Group**

ITEM	T	R	EXPLANATION
they're showing me a balance beam ... you play this role most deftly ... It is very easy to fall off, but you maintain your balance far more than most.	1	5	**A clear hit. I am aware when I am beginning to become upset and can return to center. In my workshop, I teach others to be aware of their fear reflexes, their triggers, so they may release the actions that fear generates. If we observe objectively, we can begin to see the first few minutes after we begin to become upset. I describe it as feeling as if they are off balance, tipping over**
and the peace and the love that you bring to those in your field is tangible to us.	1	6	**A super hit. I get many great reviews from my clients and see many people make significant changes in their lives.**
These words you do not need to hear for we transmit them to you mentally; at all time you are aware of our presence	1	5	**A clear hit. I am always aware of their presence, which helps.**
but perhaps it is good for you to hear them externally today for a boost of confidence and simply reunion	1	6	**A super hit. Again, one of the reasons I "called." I needed a spiritual hug**
They are showing me that there are times when you say, "Why am I not with you guys now? I'd rather be over there"	1	6	**A super hit. I have felt heartbroken and distant from them several times since my NDE.**

ITEM	T	R	EXPLANATION
but you are sort of smiling	1	1	A miss. I was weeping as she talked at this point. I had the phone muted
he feels like a free spirit	1	5	A clear hit. I am not scoring the metaphor as it is followed by what her metaphor meant. He was unique and original, unaffected and impulsive without being reckless
what I'm feeling is a very mellow presence	1	5	A clear hit. He was calm and relaxed with his life. He asked many questions about life and spirit. He loved math and would buy calculus books to read even if he wasn't in the class
Somebody who was not too easily ruffled. He's showing me "Oh, yeah, I could have a temper.	1	3	A possible fit. I never saw him lose his temper, but he was distressed when we would hear stories regarding child or animal abuse. And he was protective towards me
but there's just a chilled out feeling around him	1	5	A clear hit. She summarizes correctly
the very casual dress I want to be ... in blue jeans and something	1	6	A super hit. He always had jeans and a t-shirt, simple and relaxed
fringy Oh, no wonder, this is the seventies, like a fringy vest, like a leather vest, like a suede vest with fringes on the bottom	1	6	A super hit. He bought me a beautiful, hand-made vest with long fringe when we were visiting Santa Fe

ITEM	T	R	EXPLANATION
don't forget or be on time or you need this reminder because you are not punctual	1	2	**A stretch. I was not late but always rushing to all my classes. And I am never late now**
But you and he were like ... wow, I'm seeing like a twin flame.... that's the image that he's showing me ... so you were a couple?	1	6	**A super hit. Suzanne finally understood from the images that he had been my boyfriend, not a friend or family member**
and that you had a pact	2	4	**Probable fit. Suzanne is referring to the agreement we had to come down together and return on the same day**
and he's guiding you; he's showing me that he's been guiding you, he's one of the guides from the other side	1	5	**A clear hit. A couple of months before, it dawned on me that when he died, he had returned to our soul Group. I had never thought of it beforehand**
You'd set the date when you would be together again. That was one exit point	1	4	**A probable hit was referencing the fact that we had signed up to leave when I was 21 but that I changed my mind and stayed.**
I also see some artwork or jewelry	1	6	**A super hit. I make crystal jewelry**
You are aligning with somebody that does artwork I see, hmm	1	1	**A miss. I am not aligning with an artist nor was I a year ago**

ITEM	T	R	EXPLANATION
colorful paintings or mandalas ... open air market fair and people are just drawn to the light from all of that	1	3	**A possible fit. I do trunk shows but they are in a store, and there are no mandalas, though I do the adult coloring books of mandalas. But they are never for sale**
it feels if you may have been questioning your purpose here still, even though you know very intuitively why you're here, why you are doing the work you are doing	1	6	**A super hit. The reason I had contacted her was my feeling of drifting or ineffectiveness**
you are of course always experiencing incremental growth, more and more peace, more and more of a settled feeling and it's all perfect	1	5	**a clear hit as over the last few years, I am more and more peaceful.**
they are showing me something falling off a shelf, some object falling on the floor of its own accord, they are just acknowledging it	1	6	**A super hit. This is explained next but my shower caddy always slides down my shower when I do any type of meditation during my shower and only then**
wait a minute ... they are showing me the word and ... the trajectory, that's it, the trajectory of possibilities...okay...	1	6	**A super hit. I often use the word *trajectory* when I am working with a client. I often wonder why. It is an awkward word yet every time I try to switch to the word *arc*, a perfect substitute, I automatically go back to the word trajectory**

APPENDIX 3

Astrological Reading for the Day of Lesley Lupo's NDE, by Astrologer Johndennis Govert

I n the Metaphysical Department of Canyon Ranch, providers will often trade services with each other. It is always interesting to see things from another perspective. When Johndennis Govert started working at the ranch, we did each other's readings. He began with interpreting my chart using Chinese astrology and, at the end, switched to my I Ching astrology chart. He looked at my chart and said, "This is astonishing. How did you survive?"

When I asked him to explain, he pointed out the position of the stars and, with my I Ching hexagram, said that I should not have survived my first thirty years of life. "I cannot see how you lived past your early twenties, maybe maximum twenty-five." Since he knew nothing of my past or the NDE, I smiled inwardly and let him continue.

He then looked at the next thirty years of my life and said that, with all the vicissitudes, I must have felt tied onto a roller coaster. That was the same image I had always used to describe that period of my life.

He pointed out one particular bad downward swing in the spring of 1988 and remarked that also meant severe illness and death. I remained quiet, so he proceeded to calculate my trajectory after the age of sixty-one. The hexagram was Joy. He explained that I would now know Heaven on earth. He smiled as he clarified it was time for me to coast and enjoy life. I still had work to do, but I would experience great happiness in my inner self and my work. I asked him how long this stage would last and he calculated and then said to me, "ninety-four years old." I smiled again.

I finally told him how accurate his reading was about my past. I was supposed to die when I was twenty-one. I mentioned that I had a near-death experience in March of 1988. Intrigued, he asked me to describe it. When I got to the part of walking up to a table and standing next to Ra-u and Meena, he stopped me.

"Have you ever studied Vedic astrology?" Johndennis asked.

I had studied astrology with gifted teachers when I was in Albuquerque attending college, but I never considered the Vedic method. Once I had my chart done in India but all I could remember was that my Sun sign was not Virgo, it was in Leo. He asked me to write the specific date and time and said we would continue to talk about it the following day. He didn't want any more details. The next day he came in, extremely excited about the chart.

For those who have studied astrology and want a more detailed technical explanation of all the calculations and their intrinsic values, Johndennis Govert has written it up, weaving together all the synchronicities interspersed throughout the chart. It is methodical and precise, describing all the nuances of my NDE chart. For others, whose heads swim when they begin to read the entire astrology chart in detail, I will summarize the elements of my chart that reflected my NDE.

Two things struck me immediately. The first was that on the day I had my accident, Ra-u, which is the north node of the moon in Vedic astrology, was crossing through the constellation of Meena, which is Sanskrit for Pisces. This configuration happens roughly once every nineteen years. That surprised me; astronomical alignments like that are rare. Eleven other members of my soul group sat at the table, yet Ra-u and Meena were the two light beings that I conversed with during my entire trip. No one else spoke to me individually.

The second piece of information cleared up something that had puzzled me for many years. As Johndennis explained Ra-u position in Vedic astrology, the reason for his clothing's odd colors became crystal-clear. Ra-u's color in the color spectrum is ultraviolet, a rich and riveting purple like his shirt. In addition, those clashing orangy-brown pants represented hessonite garnet, the spiritual stone of Ra-u.

Then another mystery cleared up. As I looked at the astrology chart, I noticed a deep and pronounced "V." I know enough of astrology to know that it is not an everyday occurrence. At the top of the "V" were two planets, Jupiter and Venus. They were extremely close to each other in the Midheaven. The bottom of the "V" rested on the Nadir and there stood the planet Pluto, ruler of the Underworld—including death and dying.

Venus symbolizes the goddess or the Divine female or mother. Jupiter, the king of the gods, signifies the Divine male or father. Pluto is the god of Hades, which means that he is the lord of death. The Divine Mother and Father, the two planets that give the most blessings, had worked together to protect my journey into the underworld. John pointed out that there was a twenty-six-minute window for me to visit Hades and return relatively untouched.

Those three planets formed the deep "V" that Saraswati had drawn for me up in the Hall of Records. I now realized that the dots she had sketched were planets. At the time, I had thought it represented something like a crack in the wall that I could slip through and return.

I wondered if I should take this new information and rewrite the part of my journey Upstairs. I could expand on my meeting when I was in the Hall of Records. In the end, I decided to keep the story as is because, at the time I experienced it, I had no idea what the V represented.

Later that day, I was amazed as I examined the notes that I had scribbled. Johndennis had answered many questions that I puzzled over. However, me being me, I went online to some of the free astrology sites and plugged in the same data I had given him. The readings were different from the standard fluff one finds. All the oddities in my chart were mentioned in the three web pages I used. Two of the three sites even indicated a connection to death as a career. One recommended I should be a mortician; the other said I look into becoming a hospice worker. Those clarifications surprised me, and they directly corroborated information from my trip Upstairs.

The following chapter comprises his interpretations of the rest of the influences that were present in my NDE.

Lesley Lupo

APPENDIX 4

Persephone and the Lord of Death in Lesley Lupo's NDE Astrology

One day Lesley Lupo and I traded readings. I calculated her chart, and, as I did, without knowing, I found some odd anomalies regarding death and dying on her birth chart. Afterward, she mentioned that she had experienced a near-death experience (NDE) and so I asked her for more details. As Lesley described it, I became more and more interested in her story. I asked her if she ever studied Vedic astrology. She replied no but once, in India, she consulted with an astrologer. The only information Lesley remembered was that her sun sign differed from Western astrology.

The description of whom she met "Upstairs" intrigued me the most. Lesley approached an oval table with twelve chairs and eleven light beings. As an astrologer, I realized that she described the twelve-star constellations of the zodiac. She walked up and sat in her seat. A woman named Meena sat on her left and, on her other side, sat a man named Ra-u. Lesley heard their names, but they made no impression, other than that some of the people at the table were the same light beings she had seen as a child.

Although Vedic astrology is not my expertise, I knew enough to recognize that Meena was Sanskrit for Pisces and Ra-u, or Rahu, was Sanskrit for the north node of the moon. It is often called the "Dragon's head." I asked her for the date and time, and she wrote it down. That night I worked out Lesley's Vedic chart of her NDE.

The first odd thing I discovered was that at the precise moment she died, the shadowy planet of Rahu was crossing through the constellation of Meena. Rahu moves backward through Meena roughly every nineteen years. Somehow, and somewhere, suspended between life and death, Lesley sat and talked with the personification of a constellation and a shadow planet quite casually and familiarly.

It also explained to her why Rahu dressed in what she felt were mismatched colors. His vibrational color is ultra-violet, and his stone is hessonite garnet, an orange-colored stone.

To me, this underscores the remarkable credibility of Lesley's experience, which occurred at what Carl Jung would call an archetypical level. This astrological exploration views the many layers of meaning embedded in Lesley's NDE. It amplifies much of what Lesley has described in her book.

The stars speak in symbols that I have grouped to present the themes in both Lesley's birth and NDE charts. Planets and their angles of connection, i.e., signs, houses, stars, and asteroids, often overlap. When we realize the whole picture, we can see that the same celestial themes reflect our life stories. This idea reveals itself in Lesley's two charts as well as her biography to date.

An astrology chart forms a circular image, a mandala if you will, which displays how the sky and earth relate to each other at any precise moment. It is not based on linear logic; it is a cyclic and spiral reasoning. What follows is a description of the starry and mythic links that reflect Lesley's personal story and how they fit together in a comprehensive view.

I looked into the mirror of the heavens, both for her birth chart and for the astrological chart of the NDE moment: in other words, her death chart. Revived ten to twelve minutes later, Lesley's astrology chart of that moment created a new birth, or even rebirth, chart. Between the time she died and the time she returned, the earth revolved just four degrees. I wanted to understand the greater magnitude of what happened then and continues to unfold for Lesley.

Let's start with the astrology everyone knows. In Lesley's birth chart, her sun sign is Virgo. To the Romans, Virgo did not mean virgins the way Western cultures now define it. Instead, it referred to young women, maidens of childbearing age who bring forth another wave of life and raise the next generation of children. The Sun in Virgo endows its natives with an intellectual and practical mind expressed in both analytical organization and a talent for everyday engineering.

The so-named "star of destiny" for anyone born in Virgo is Mercury, which is the heavenly messenger and mediator. One of Mercury's features is to be able to intercede, to arbitrate, and, in doing so, build a foundation for mutual understanding between people of opposing viewpoints. Because Mercury is the messenger, it can go "between worlds," i.e., from life on earth into Hades, the place of death, and return untouched.

Virgo and its opposite sign, Pisces, are the two signs that indicate selfless service to others whether it happens in the sphere of family and friends or farther away in the outer community or the international community.

In everyone's chart the planets, signs, and houses represent our active karma, the accumulation of all the thoughts and deeds we have ever created. Karmic lessons usually work out themselves slowly and release any struggles associated with them over the course of many lifetimes. In keeping with this karmic unfolding, the practice of yoga takes the astrology signs and matches them up into six different pairs. Female and male signs ruled by the same planet form the core of our human chakras. Imagine two signs on either side of each chakra situated up the spine.

If these two opposites have a strong interaction with each other, it causes one's karma to collapse, which directs energy into our central spinal column. As our karma collapses, so do the difficulties associated with said karma. Karma collapse can happen in two ways: the first is from the result of advanced yoga or meditative practice. The other way is death.

Lesley suffered the traumatic accident that caused her NDE. She died and returned when the Sun was in Pisces, which lies directly opposite her original birth sun sign Virgo. For Lesley, the opposite energies of Virgo and Pisces collapsed into her central spinal channel. This allowed her struggles to disappear as well. From that date on, any and all karmic blocks dissolved.

While a grounded Virgo represents a practical earth sign, Pisces, by contrast, symbolizes an intuitive water sign ruled by Neptune. Both Pisces and Neptune bring a close relationship to the fields of mysticism, art, and music. Interestingly, both planet and constellation overlap: they both rule and influence the same world items as well. These things relate to Lesley's NDE experience: large animals (horses), comas, hospitals, and both foggy perception as well as an increase in psychic abilities. It is uncanny in how the chart describes her accident and recovery.

On her NDE chart, five of her ten planets are in the sign of Capricorn and that emphasizes the theme of balancing common sense with mysticism. In most charts, planets scatter throughout the astrology chart. Here they not only concentrate on one side, the western hemisphere, but half of her planets sit in one sign. This rare planetary cluster is crucial for her.

All of the planets in Lesley's NDE chart fall in the half circle on the western side. When one-half of the circle is full and the other half is empty, it is called a "bowl chart." As a rule, bowl charts are unusual and will be north, south, east, or west. When the planets all cluster in the western hemisphere bowl, it indicates how significant others are to her. Western bowl people can take on activities initiated by others, brainstorming to finish the project. Considering the needs of others affects their action since their focus is on serving others. They must be reminded to take care of themselves.

People with bowl charts also become examples to their generation about whatever issue the planets signify. Lesley's birth is during the twenty years between 1940 and 1960. Venus joined with Jupiter, and both are opposite to Pluto, so this Baby Boomer generation will look to see how she resolved the question of life after life, or, life after rebirth. They want to know how she pragmatically incorporated this matter into her day-to-day living. Moreover, instead of blindly following, they will want to know how they may gain the same certainty she displays.

Uranus and Saturn start the group. Saturn represents constriction, old age, and responsibility. Uranus represents freedom, revolution, reformation, and innovation. Two planets with extremely opposite qualities sit right next to each other, and both exert the same amount of influence in Lesley's life. Her challenge is to bring the opposing forces into harmony and make them work as a pair to balance change: change that happens not for the sake of upheaval but happens for constructive growth.

The third planet is Neptune, and that indicates intuition. Capricorn (and its ruler Saturn) represents destiny, karma, and solid construction. The positions of Neptune and Saturn, in both Lesley's birth and NDE charts, separate from each other by just a few degrees, so the energies of two planets meld powerfully to influence her charts. That is significant because these two planets join one another about every thirty-six years, which is the exact age when Lesley experienced her NDE. To have her original birthday and her NDE with the same planetary influences is highly improbable—and important.

These two planets gave Lesley strong psychic abilities as she began her life. They also presented her capacity to understand subtle perceptions in a practical, easy-to-understand manner. The NDE amplified her original talents and, at the same time, re-emphasized her role as a bridge between the worlds. She can easily see, hear, and feel what remains just outside the perception of most people.

These powerful opposites joined, which indicates another theme for Lesley. She now works and contributes toward opening the spiritual view of humans. In the physical sciences, the materialist theory is that when the body dies so does the soul or any awareness. However, the science world is now shifting to a post-materialist concept. Consciousness is changing, which started in the mid-1800s. It began to transfer from the domain of philosophers to the studies of scientists. Lesley speaks to this change by integrating a scientific and a spiritual perspective.

During the NDE, Lesley discovered she had "jumped her contract" and chose to stay on earth. However, she was offered the choice to pursue one of two different purposes: one was to go back to earth and the other was to stay "Upstairs." Her decision to return established a new foundation and reshaped her destiny.

The last two planets in the Capricorn cluster are Mars and the Moon. I will defer discussion of the NDE Moon in Capricorn for a few more paragraphs to connect it with another theme. Mars is "exalted" which means it is particularly well placed when it passes through the sign of Capricorn, so all the Moon's attributes become heightened. Mars is the planet of daring and action. It will function with greater perseverance and produce longer lasting effects as it moves through Capricorn. In addition, when Mars is next to Neptune, it tugs at and brings the subconscious realms up to the conscious mind, which make them accessible. This celestial combination further boosts Lesley's psychic gifts and increases her ability to articulate whatever subtle world insights she receives more practically. In other words, she can peek behind the veil and not be so overwhelmed by what she sees that she cannot share it in a way that most people can understand.

To many mystical traditions, having a positive death experience is both a blessing and a remarkable spiritual opportunity. Jupiter rules positive deaths, and, in both Lesley's birth and NDE charts, Jupiter, prominently placed, indicates natural life-to-death transitions.

The accident that caused her injury and subsequent hospital stay may not sound very beneficial, but she did not suffer any severe incapacitating effects from the stampede. In addition, as you listen to Lesley's story in her words, there is extraordinary clarity in the detailed sensory descriptions she provides. Her mind was lucid and awake, instantly aware of the new surroundings in the NDE. She perceived at that moment, and later as she re-occupied her body, an expansive and open philosophical view that recognized the good fortune in what initially seemed liked unfortunate circumstances. These are qualities of Jupiter.

In Lesley's NDE chart, Jupiter and Venus stand next to each other at the highest point of the diagram. Directly below, 180 degrees away from the lowest point, the dark planet Pluto, the god of the underworld (which means that he is the lord of death), opposes the positions of Venus and Jupiter. Venus symbolizes the goddess, the Divine female who brings beauty, harmony, bounty, and love. Jupiter, as king of the gods, symbolizes the Divine male and represents the beneficial order of secular authority as it expands beyond present boundaries. The Divine Mother and Father worked together to protect her journey into the underworld for the twenty-six minutes that the planets were in that configuration.

However, more than this, when Lesley was Upstairs with Saraswati and asked why she had returned at that time, she was shown a deep "V" with little solid circles at both the ends and the angle of the "V." She thought it was a crack in the fabric of Being that she was somehow able to slip through. When she first saw the chart, she told me how stunned she was. These three planets comprised the extreme "V" she had witnessed.

Pluto also rules anything hidden in the dark. Pluto is likely to be extremely active in any chart concerning death, such as an NDE horoscope. The prominence of Jupiter and Venus is a blessing to Lesley and a blessing to others through Lesley. Pluto's presence indicates that her abilities to benefit others can arise quickly as a medium, an NDE researcher, or counselor and teacher about the process of death, dying, and transition to the next phase. In her chart, Pluto is emphasized by sitting right next to Mercury the communicator. The lord of the underworld actively and powerfully communicates with Lesley. She became a magnet for the teachings about what happens in the shadows when humans cross the river separating the living from the dead and enter Pluto's realm. She can bring back messages from that domain.

Next, I want to point out that the Moon was in Capricorn in a grouping of five planets in that same constellation in Lesley's NDE chart. The moon represents women, especially mothers. Capricorn is the third of the earth signs. Taurus, the first earth sign, suggests planting crops in spring; Virgo's concerns are gathering the bounty of the harvest in autumn, and Capricorn feeds on the stored bounty of food through the long cold winter. In Capricorn, the mother is both aged and wise.

The storyline of the Roman myth of the earth mother goddess Ceres (goddess of agriculture) and her daughter Proserpine mimic many themes in Lesley's NDE. In the tale, Amor, the son of Venus, shot Pluto with his arrows of love and enchantment. Pluto saw Proserpine bathing and playing at a lake. Pluto seized her and took her to the underworld. Ceres discovered her daughter Proserpine missing and conducted a worldwide search for her. Not finding her daughter, in despair, anger, and revenge, Ceres stopped nurturing plants and life. The land she walked on turned into a desert.

Gods and humans alike petitioned Jupiter for a solution. Jupiter learned that his brother Pluto abducted Proserpine and had taken her to the underworld where none wished to enter, and almost none returned. Jupiter dispatched Mercury to negotiate a settlement with Pluto. Both sides tried to use trickery, but the final agreement called for Proserpine to spend four months a year in the underworld as Pluto's wife. After that, she returned to her mother for the rest the year. When Proserpine left to visit the underworld, Ceres brought winter and allowed plants to die. After Proserpine had returned to her mother, Ceres renewed the life cycle and created the growth of crops and the harvests that supported all.

This also appears in Lesley's NDE chart. Another feature of the moon in Capricorn is when Ceres embodies the mother who can bring about either bounty or barrenness. Proserpine is another visage of Virgo, the maiden whose life entwines with planting and harvesting in each following cycle. Pluto is the judge of the world of the dead who allows everyone into his realm at some point but permits very few to return. Lesley, like Proserpine, is one of the rare ones allowed to come back and speak openly about her underworld experiences.

Mercury and Pluto strongly connect in Lesley's birth chart, and we find Mercury as the direct mediator with Pluto in the Ceres/Proserpine myth. Even more remarkable, we discover that the asteroid/dwarf planet Ceres is within one degree of Mercury in Lesley's NDE chart. The importance of the Ceres/Proserpine myth to Lesley's life path directly encodes in Lesley's vocation and future.

As Lesley and I discussed this myth, more connections appeared but not from astrology. This tale had fascinated Lesley as a child. Moreover, interestingly, since Lesley is of Sicilian descent, when I initially discussed this myth I used the Latin names as introduced above. Lesley, to my surprise, immediately used the Greek names of Demeter and Persephone instead of Ceres and Proserpine. At first, I thought this odd, but I found an old thread of connection.

Before becoming part of the Roman Empire, Sicily was part of Magna Graecia or the culture of Greater Greece. At Enna, in the middle of Sicily, lies the principal and oldest temple to Demeter and Persephone. Only priestesses served this temple: women who were also initiates and teachers of a mystical tradition of spiritual development.

The Roman version of the Persephone myth centers on Sicily as the location where it took place. Pluto emerged from the fiery depths of the Mount Aetna volcano to abduct Persephone. Demeter in her despair cursed the land of Sicily and ruined its agricultural bounty until Persephone came home. Rome eventually imported the Demeter and Persephone religious practice from Sicily to an especially built temple on Rome's Aventine Hill. The Romans bent the imported Greek religion to accommodate Roman values, but the ordinary citizenry embraced the Demeter-Persephone spiritual practices rather than privileged patrician class.

At the start of this astrological exploration, we met Rahu in the sign of Meena. Rahu is also known as the dragon's head and connects intimately with eclipses. Rahu represents the north node or a point in space where the Moon ascends northward above the equator in an arc that extends outward into space. In Vedic astrology, Rahu is usually considered malefic. It often collapses one's world during its active period only later to regenerate that same world on a higher, more spiritual footing. It is like a cycle of birth, death, and rebirth.

In Western astrology, the dragon's head reveals the evolutionary arc of an individual over many lifetimes. In that sense, Rahu refers to a remarkable destiny that unfolds and is measured in millennia. Another Rahu connection is that Lesley was born just nine days after a total solar eclipse and her NDE occurred only five days before a subsequent total solar eclipse. Astrologically, eclipses connected to the sky position of Rahu magnify the significance of events around the time they happen. Eclipses both activate and increase the scale of events they influence both positively and negatively. The two total solar eclipses in both birth and NDE charts are yet another indicator of the magnitude of Lesley's life work, which became exploring the journey of consciousness from life in a human body to living in other states of being. I think you can understand this in Lesley's story.

As time moves on, Lesley brings more of the positive influences of Rahu's intervention into the world.

The yoga of dying, death, and rebirth is called the Bardo Thodol and is more commonly known as the *Tibetan Book of the Dead*. For over thirty years I have studied this Bardo yoga and used the knowledge to interpret modern life. People in Tibet who experience NDEs are called *delogs* which means "returners from beyond." They passed through the gate of life to the world of the dead and returned with some resolve to finish important work. Often they came back to share their awareness as well as accurate information about the nature of death and dying both as a process and a state of being. Lesley is one of a growing community of American and Western *delogs* whose collective experiences are re-framing our perception of what happens to consciousness when our bodies die, but we do not.

As this book goes to press and then on to the public, there is one more improbable but necessary connecting thread from the heavens. It has to do with double timing and the voice of Rahu.

In Vedic astrology, there are nine *dashas*, or cycles, in our lives that are calculated to span over a 120-year lifespan. Each period has nine *buktis* or sub-cycles, yet the sequences and sub-cycles do not distribute symmetrically: the *buktis* unfold into different lengths of time throughout our lives. Everyone's astrological patterns are different.

As we discussed earlier, Lesley has two astrology charts, her physical birth, and her re-birth after meeting Ra-u/Rahu and Meena "Upstairs." Right now, the first cycle of Rahu and sub-cycle of Mercury are active and synchronized in both her charts. At first, that might not seem so remarkable. The cycles and sub-cycles, however, can start anywhere in the 120-year progression depending on the exact moon position over ten days. The probability of this happening is about once every 6,700 times.

This book's message is more notable than a chance event. The Mercury sub-cycle is the time when Rahu's lesson comes from the high astral worlds through Lesley's life and words into your awareness. Twice invoked, this precious book is meant to speak to you.

Johndennis Govert Dec 15th, 2015

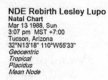

NDE Rebirth Lesley Lupo
Natal Chart
Mar 13 1988, Sun
3:07 pm MST +7:00
Tucson, Arizona
32°N13'18" 110°W55'33"
Geocentric
Tropical
Placidus
Mean Node

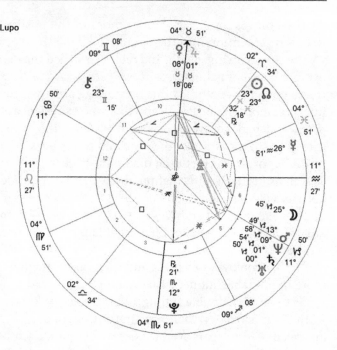

ACKNOWLEDGMENTS

My thanks go out to the many people who have shaped this manuscript. Susan Kovacs, always my first reader, who encourages and assists me with her thoughtful comments. Joey Hoffman, Jackie Vanacek, and Evie Binder took on the tedious job of reading the meandering first draft from start to finish and highlighted anything that needed a more in-depth description.

A particular second thank you to Dana Patterson for being my spirit sister and helping me weave together all the shattered parts of Spirit and human consciousness throughout the years that we have known each other. Her sound advice and humor helped me to keep everything in perspective as I was trying to put all the pieces back together after the injury. In addition, thanks for bringing me to IANDS.

I thank Chuck Swedrock and Susan Amsden and the entire AZIANDS family in Tucson for giving me a place in which I felt safe enough to open up and share, which ultimately gave me the confidence to speak about it. In addition, Susan, thanks for believing in this book, and giving me all the support that enabled me to write the book which needed to be written.

I also thank Suzanne Giesemann and Pat Bruckman who helped me to get messages from Upstairs when I couldn't receive them myself. And to Johndennis Govert, a hearty thank you for showing the fantastic way in which the Universe supports the facts.

To Dr. Kenneth Ring, I am sending a warm thank you for all of your inspiration, which spanned a critique of the rough and tumble first draft to countless and lengthy emails in which we have discussed the universe. I will post a big hug and another jar of honey. We share a passion for sports, and I swear he will be a Chicago Cubs fan before long! I promise to convert him. To become a bagpipes connoisseur might take a bit more time.

A very special thanks to Dr. Gary Schwartz for his time, friendship, and open discussion think-tanks. His boost gave me the fuel I needed to complete the tedious, time-consuming manuscript. He mentored me in the way all good ones do, a question here, and introduction there, all the while cheering me on to accomplish my goals.

I want to thank the Canyon Ranch Resort, Mel and Enid Zuckerman and Jerry Cohen, and all the people that created and continue to sustain it. They have built a sacred space where scores of spiritual people can work and be not only cherished but also treated with respect. In addition, a big hug goes out to all my clients/friends from Canyon Ranch who supported me in my pursuit of a finish to this book.

Thanks also to John Audette and Eternea for helping me to connect with like-minded people all over the world. His passion to change people's perception of death and dying are exemplary. I know his commitment to his quest will never falter.

Thanks to Elizabeth Hare for her editorial guidance. She has an artist's touch, indeed, and helped to render a fluid and flowing account of my journey.

Valuable and constructive suggestions given by Scott Miner have been a great help. His willingness to give his time so generously is much appreciated, as was his encouragement to continue to seek a publisher with whom I would develop rapport.

A hug and deep appreciation to Beatriz Labrada. During the four months I recuperated, her tireless care of me and my children helped reduce their trauma to a more manageable bump.

Last, and certainly not least, I thank Bruce Genaro, an editor par excellence who brought a level of finesse and polish to the book that I could never have captured by myself. He edited this book deftly and sympathetically. The kindness, creativity, and patience he used with my writing stayed constant. It is always a pleasure to work with you, Bruce.

I could not be who I am today without all their love, playfulness, and support.

Paperbacks also available from
White Crow Books

Elsa Barker—*Letters from
a Living Dead Man*
ISBN 978-1-907355-83-7

Elsa Barker—*War Letters from
the Living Dead Man*
ISBN 978-1-907355-85-1

Elsa Barker—*Last Letters from
the Living Dead Man*
ISBN 978-1-907355-87-5

Richard Maurice Bucke—
Cosmic Consciousness
ISBN 978-1-907355-10-3

Arthur Conan Doyle—
The Edge of the Unknown
ISBN 978-1-907355-14-1

Arthur Conan Doyle—
The New Revelation
ISBN 978-1-907355-12-7

Arthur Conan Doyle—
The Vital Message
ISBN 978-1-907355-13-4

Arthur Conan Doyle with
Simon Parke—*Conversations
with Arthur Conan Doyle*
ISBN 978-1-907355-80-6

Meister Eckhart with Simon Parke—
Conversations with Meister Eckhart
ISBN 978-1-907355-18-9

D. D. Home—*Incidents in my Life Part 1*
ISBN 978-1-907355-15-8

Mme. Dunglas Home; edited,
with an Introduction, by Sir
Arthur Conan Doyle—*D. D.
Home: His Life and Mission*
ISBN 978-1-907355-16-5

Edward C. Randall—
Frontiers of the Afterlife
ISBN 978-1-907355-30-1

Rebecca Ruter Springer—
Intra Muros: My Dream of Heaven
ISBN 978-1-907355-11-0

Leo Tolstoy, edited by Simon
Parke—*Forbidden Words*
ISBN 978-1-907355-00-4

Leo Tolstoy—*A Confession*
ISBN 978-1-907355-24-0

Leo Tolstoy—*The Gospel in Brief*
ISBN 978-1-907355-22-6

Leo Tolstoy—*The Kingdom
of God is Within You*
ISBN 978-1-907355-27-1

Leo Tolstoy—*My Religion:
What I Believe*
ISBN 978-1-907355-23-3

Leo Tolstoy—*On Life*
ISBN 978-1-907355-91-2

Leo Tolstoy—*Twenty-three Tales*
ISBN 978-1-907355-29-5

Leo Tolstoy—*What is Religion
and other writings*
ISBN 978-1-907355-28-8

Leo Tolstoy—*Work While
Ye Have the Light*
ISBN 978-1-907355-26-4

Leo Tolstoy—*The Death of Ivan Ilyich*
ISBN 978-1-907661-10-5

Leo Tolstoy—*Resurrection*
ISBN 978-1-907661-09-9

Leo Tolstoy with Simon Parke—
Conversations with Tolstoy
ISBN 978-1-907355-25-7

Howard Williams with an Introduction
by Leo Tolstoy—*The Ethics of Diet:
An Anthology of Vegetarian Thought*
ISBN 978-1-907355-21-9

Vincent Van Gogh with Simon Parke—
Conversations with Van Gogh
ISBN 978-1-907355-95-0

Wolfgang Amadeus Mozart with Simon
Parke—*Conversations with Mozart*
ISBN 978-1-907661-38-9

Jesus of Nazareth with Simon Parke—
Conversations with Jesus of Nazareth
ISBN 978-1-907661-41-9

Thomas à Kempis with Simon
Parke—*The Imitation of Christ*
ISBN 978-1-907661-58-7

Julian of Norwich with Simon
Parke—*Revelations of Divine Love*
ISBN 978-1-907661-88-4

Allan Kardec—*The Spirits Book*
ISBN 978-1-907355-98-1

Allan Kardec—*The Book on Mediums*
ISBN 978-1-907661-75-4

Emanuel Swedenborg—*Heaven and Hell*
ISBN 978-1-907661-55-6

P.D. Ouspensky—*Tertium Organum:
The Third Canon of Thought*
ISBN 978-1-907661-47-1

Dwight Goddard—*A Buddhist Bible*
ISBN 978-1-907661-44-0

Michael Tymn—*The Afterlife Revealed*
ISBN 978-1-970661-90-7

Michael Tymn—*Transcending the
Titanic: Beyond Death's Door*
ISBN 978-1-908733-02-3

Guy L. Playfair—*If This Be Magic*
ISBN 978-1-907661-84-6

Guy L. Playfair—*The Flying Cow*
ISBN 978-1-907661-94-5

Guy L. Playfair —*This House is Haunted*
ISBN 978-1-907661-78-5

Carl Wickland, M.D.—
Thirty Years Among the Dead
ISBN 978-1-907661-72-3

John E. Mack—*Passport to the Cosmos*
ISBN 978-1-907661-81-5

Peter & Elizabeth Fenwick—
The Truth in the Light
ISBN 978-1-908733-08-5

Erlendur Haraldsson—
Modern Miracles
ISBN 978-1-908733-25-2

Erlendur Haraldsson—
At the Hour of Death
ISBN 978-1-908733-27-6

Erlendur Haraldsson—
The Departed Among the Living
ISBN 978-1-908733-29-0

Brian Inglis—*Science and Parascience*
ISBN 978-1-908733-18-4

Brian Inglis—*Natural and Supernatural:
A History of the Paranormal*
ISBN 978-1-908733-20-7

Ernest Holmes—*The Science of Mind*
ISBN 978-1-908733-10-8

Victor & Wendy Zammit —*A Lawyer
Presents the Evidence For the Afterlife*
ISBN 978-1-908733-22-1

Casper S. Yost—*Patience
Worth: A Psychic Mystery*
ISBN 978-1-908733-06-1

William Usborne Moore—
Glimpses of the Next State
ISBN 978-1-907661-01-3

William Usborne Moore—
The Voices
ISBN 978-1-908733-04-7

John W. White—
The Highest State of Consciousness
ISBN 978-1-908733-31-3

Stafford Betty—
The Imprisoned Splendor
ISBN 978-1-907661-98-3

Paul Pearsall, Ph.D. —
Super Joy
ISBN 978-1-908733-16-0

All titles available as eBooks, and selected titles available in Hardback and Audiobook formats from www.whitecrowbooks.com

CPSIA information can be obtained
at www.ICGtesting.com
Printed in the USA
BVHW032357061119
563155BV00003B/331/P